Sin and Judgment in the Prophets

SOCIETY OF BIBLICAL LITERATURE

MONOGRAPH SERIES

James L. Crenshaw, Editor

NUMBER 27

SIN AND JUDGMENT IN THE PROPHETS

A Stylistic and Theological Analysis

by

Patrick D. Miller, Jr.

PATRICK D. MILLER, JR.

SIN AND JUDGMENT IN THE PROPHETS

A Stylistic and Theological Analysis

SCHOLARS PRESS

Published by
Scholars Press
101 Salem St.
P. O. Box 2268
Chico, CA 95927

SIN AND JUDGMENT IN THE PROPHETS
A Stylistic and Theological Analysis
by
Patrick D. Miller, Jr.

Library of Congress Cataloging in Publication Data

Miller, Patrick D.
Sin and judgment in the prophets.

(Society of Biblical Literature monograph series ; no. 27) (ISSN 0145-269X)
Bibliography: p.
1. Sin—Biblical teaching. 2. Judgment of God—Biblical teaching. 3. Bible. O.T. Prophets—Criticism, interpretation, etc. I. Title. II. Series.
BS1199.S54M54 231.7 81-8950
ISBN 0-89130-514-9 AACR2
ISBN 0-89130-515-7 (pbk.)

Printed in the United States of America

To Mary Ann

TABLE OF CONTENTS

Preface

The nature and mode of divine judgment are concerns of no small moment in the Judaeo-Christian tradition. Within that tradition the prophets of Israel are among the principal bearers and interpreters of the word of judgment and its relationship to human activity. Any treatment of the prophets and their message will obviously deal with this subject. But the topic is large enough, important enough, and sufficiently problematic that it needs some fresh thinking and study apart from general surveys of the prophets or prophetic theology. The following chapters are offered as a part of that larger study by focusing on one aspect of the subject, the correlation of sin and judgment in prophetic oracles and narratives with attention to both stylistic and theological dimension, to see how the two are united in a single whole.

This monograph had its inception in a paper read to a meeting of the Colloquium for Biblical Research. Parts of it were read to Old Testament Seminars at the Universities of Cambridge, Oxford, Manchester, Nottingham, and Sheffield as well as Kings College, London. I am indebted to all my hosts and friends on those occasions and the often vigorous discussion that helped me sharpen and correct my thinking. My colleague and good friend, W. Sibley Towner, who has shared a continuing interest in the questions of divine justice and judgment, read the entire manuscript and provided helpful and stimulating criticism. At the same time, he graciously offered to lighten my teaching load during the time that I was finishing this project. The influence of my senior colleague, James L. Mays, who both personally and by his writings has always been my mentor, will be immediately apparent to anyone who even peruses these pages.

Much of the preparation of this book was carried out during a sabbatical year in England. I am indebted to Union Theological Seminary in Virginia for granting me that year of study consistent with its long-standing tradition of supporting the theological scholarship carried on by its faculty. A grant from the Association of Theological Schools provided additional financial assistance during that period.

I am grateful to James L. Crenshaw of Vanderbilt Divinity School for his helpful editing.

ABBREVIATIONS

ANET	*Ancient Near Eastern Texts Relating to the Old Testament*
BDB	Brown, Driver, and Briggs, *A Hebrew and English Lexicon of the Old Testament*
BH^3	*Biblia Hebraica* (3rd edition)
BHS	*Biblia Hebraica Stuttgartensis*
BKAT	Biblischer Kommentar, Altes Testament
BZAW	Beihefte zur ZAW
CAD	*Chicago Assyrian Dictionary*
CBQ	*Catholic Biblical Quarterly*
HAT	Handbuch zum Alten Testament
HKAT	Handkommentar zum Alten Testament
HUCA	*Hebrew Union College Annual*
ICC	International Critical Commentary
JANES	*Journal of the Ancient Near Eastern Society of Columbia University*
JTS	*Journal of Theological Studies*
KAT	*Kommentar zum Alten Testament*
LXX	Septuagint
MT	Massoretic Text
SBL	Society of Biblical Literature
ThLZ	*Theologische Literaturzeitung*
VT	*Vetus Testamentum*
WMANT	Wissenschaftliche Monographien zum Alten und Neuen Testament
ZAW	*Zeitschrift für die Alttestamentliche Wissenschaft*
ZThK	*Zeitschrift für Theologie und Kirche*

Introduction

Yahweh has a lawsuit with Judah
    and will punish Jacob according to his ways;
        according to his deeds he will turn back to him.

Hos 12:3

As you have done, it shall be done to you
    Your deed (g^e*mûl*) shall return on your head.

Obad 15

Expressions similar to these verses from Hosea and Obadiah occur elsewhere in the prophets (e.g. Isa 3:11; Jer 6:19; 21:14; Hos 4:9; Joel 4:4) and point to the subject under consideration in these pages. My intention is to explore the extent to which and the way in which the prophetic understanding of the relationship between sin and judgment suggested by the above texts is spelled out or articulated in various ways in the proclamation of the prophets. This essay therefore is a study of the device/pattern/motif[1] of *correspondence* between sin and judgment, crime and punishment, that is, the prophetic announcement that punishment will be according to, in some way like, or appropriate in either a literal or symbolic fashion to the sin committed. The subject matter is thus somewhat more narrow than the title indicates. The notion of judgment in the prophets needs continual reexamination and interpretation from various aspects. The dimension of correspondence is only one of those but understanding its nature and function may help one better comprehend the larger picture.

As the subtitle suggests, this study is concerned with both *stylistic* and *theological* aspects of correspondence. The correlation of sin and judgment is one of the ways in which the prophet speaks about judgment. Examination of the manifold examples of correspondence helps to understand the complex shape of prophetic rhetoric and style in at least one area. When the prophets made some correlation between sin and judgment, it was done with great variety. Very few examples are alike. Yet one can discern recurring ways of indicating that correspondence and give a kind of typology of those

[1] Any of these terms could be used. The correspondence is clearly a pattern of speech and/or a rhetorical device in the prophets. It also represents a motif within the prophetic word of judgment.

ways. (See chapters I & III.) But patterns of rhetoric or speaking are always vehicles of communication. So any analysis of style eventually presses into questions of meaning. What is the function of this correspondence? What do the prophets intend or accomplish by it? What part does it play in the prophetic theology of judgment? (See chapters I & IV.)

The presence or use of a pattern of correspondence that conveys among other things irony and poetic justice has long been recognized or pointed out, often however, as a passing observation or in discussion of a particular text. There have been some more extended examinations of this correspondence. Several of those which have appeared over the last decades provide a base upon which a more inclusive study may be built.

In 1934 Hans Walter Wolff produced a comprehensive treatment of the motivations or reasons in prophetic salvation and judgment sayings.[2] As a part of that study he devoted several pages to what he saw as an inner connection between the reason (*Begründung*) and what was announced for the future because of it. He saw in the examples analyzed several ways of understanding that relationship: the later event as the inevitable consequence or out-growth of prior actions within the nexus of human intra-mundane events; a causal connection of a direct sort that is rooted in Yahweh's righteousness so that Yahweh acts as the direct consequence of an action against him; a contrasting of the state of affairs wherein Yahweh's will to punish connects what is not connected in the sense of seed which grows into harvest; a strict parallel of actions in reason and announcement; ironic parallel or reversal of the action in the movement from reason to announcement; and the will of the people set against Yahweh's will so that Yahweh announces that what the people have denied as a possibility will happen to them. Wolff also indicates that it is not necessary for the sin and the judgment to be related at all. He then suggests a kind of inner-stylistic typology of how these varying relationships are expressed. Most of these are variations of the pattern of repeating the same words in both the accusation and the announcement of judgment. Wolff sees a kind of spectrum or gradation from exactly corresponding actions indicated by the same words to exactly reversed actions in which what is spoken of in the accusation is ironically reversed in the judgment. In between one will find cases where the parallel word takes on new meaning or is given another content by different or contrasting words associated with it. Another stylistic category is found in the use of comparison sayings to underscore the logical connection, e.g. seed harvest (Hos 8:7). Sometimes an extended metaphor may express the close relationship of sin and judgment.

[2] H. W. Wolff, "Die Begründung der prophetischen Heils und Unheilssprüche," *ZAW* 52 (1934) 1–22. (Reprinted in *Gesammelte Studien zum Alten Testament* (München: Kaiser, 1973) 9–35.

Wolff's analysis opens the way for a more extended and inclusive typology of the correspondence sayings. He has used only a few of them to work out his schema. A broader investigation will lead to some refinements in his helpful treatment and will suggest both that some of his categories actually fall together (e.g. his varying forms of word repetition) while other categories need to be included (e.g. indirect correspondence that has to do with the instrument of sin).

Before leaving Wolff it should be noted that in his treatment of various passages in Hosea in his commentary[3] he has contributed important further insights, particularly his discernment of the *Talionstil* in Hosea.

Claus Westermann in his basic study of the judgment speech in Old Testament prophecy has also pointed to the correspondence pattern as an element in some judgment speeches.[4] He cites a few examples but concludes that he cannot answer the question about the origin and meaning of this motif.

Shortly after Westermann's work appeared, Norbert Lohfink proposed an answer to that question in an essay on Hos 4:4–6.[5] While this article deals with only one passage, Lohfink gives considerable attention to the repetition of the *Tätigkeitsworte*. He starts from Wolff's conclusion that in Hos 4:4–6 one encounters a *Talionstil*. Lohfink argues that this is not exactly the case. Unlike Hos 4:4–6 which is dependent on parallel verbs, the talion formula is formed nominally: "eye for eye", "life for life". It also is not independent but is inserted in a legal sentence. That is true even when it occurs in a prophetic judgment speech (1 Kgs 20:42), though Lohfink acknowledges it is possible for the talion formula to be developed into a full legal sentence with action words, as for example in Gen 9:6a.

Although Lohfink sees distinctions between talion formulas and the style of Hos 4:4ff., he does not mean that there are no talionic notions here. Rather, he reaches two basic conclusions:

> (1) The talion formulas and Hos 4:5f. are only two points within a wider field of forms and expressions in which *Talionsdenken* is expressed through repetition of words.
>
> (2) Within the genre of the prophetic announcement of judgment one often finds the repetition of the action word so that one can probably speak of it as a typical (if also optional) element of the genre.

Within that broader field of *Talionsdenken* Lohfink finds repetition of verbs of action in curse formulas protecting memorial inscriptions and treaties (e.g. Kilamuwa, Karatepe, and Sefire inscriptions). One also finds it in the sacral legal process as indicated by Josh 7. This text points Lohfink to

[3] H. W. Wolff, *Hosea* (Hermeneia; Philadelphia: Fortress Press, 1974) *passim*.

[4] C. Westermann, *Basic Forms of Prophetic Speech* (Philadelphia: Westminster, 1967) 160–61.

[5] N. Lohfink, "Zu Text und Form von Os 4, 4–6," *Biblica* 42 (1961) 303–32.

what he sees as the true setting of this way of speaking: the covenant. In the diplomatic correspondence and international treaties of the ancient Near East there is a "parity style" involving the repetition of verbs of action describing what both parties are to do or not to do. The clause of reciprocal duties of protection frequently gives repeated activity words, and that style element could be taken over out of the middle part of the treaty, which contained the conditions, into the concluding section of blessings and curses. That "parity style" then presumably came over into the language and form of covenant between Yahweh and Israel. Not surprisingly we find it now in Hosea, which demonstrates other close affinities to covenant language and forms. One may conclude that the connection of sin and judgment through repetition of verbs belongs to the parity style in the covenant tradition. After citing several passages, mostly in the historical books, that suggest a covenant association Lohfink concludes in summary that the repeated action words of Hos 4:5 echo in part the talion formulas, in part curse forms and capital judgments; it is a style element which enters earlier in prophetic judgment speeches to individuals, showing its connection to the covenant tradition there and in Hos 4:4–6. In almost all its dimensions it manifests legal judicial associations.

Along with that of Wolff, Lohfink's study represents the most important recent work on this subject, especially with regard to the setting and origin of some basic modes of correspondence. His focus is entirely on the form of correspondence that takes place through repeated verbs. As Wolff has already discerned, that is a basic category. But there are other ways in which the prophets correlate judgment with sin that need to be taken into consideration for a full understanding of this dimension of the prophet's message and its style. While the connection of the correspondence pattern to the covenant tradition may not be as direct as Lohfink seems to suggest—and it must be said not all of his connections to covenant formulations are very direct—there are connections and we shall point to some others. His discernment of the talionic notions inherent in the particular form of correspondence he investigates is correct. Indeed one can go further than Lohfink in relating some of the prophetic correspondences to actual talionic formulations (see chapter III).

Three other works may be mentioned more briefly. In a section under the heading "Reversal of Imagery" Waldemar Janzen has looked at the phenomenon of correspondence briefly, and primarily by way of summary and discussion of Lohfink's essay.[6] Janzen's principal contribution is in noting the prevalence of the correspondence device in *hôy*-pericopes or woe-sayings. It may be said that this rhetorical mode is just as much an element in the *hôy* woe saying as in the judgment speech but that is because in so many instances the woe saying comprises the accusation of the judgment

[6] W. Janzen, *Mourning Cry and Woe Oracle* (BZAW 125; Berlin: de Gruyter, 1972).

speech. These oracles will be discussed in the next chapter with one or two additions to Janzen's list.

Two articles by Fichtner[7] and Zimmerli[8] have examined in detail the character of Isaiah's prophetic speech with some attention to the correspondence pattern there. We shall draw upon their works, particularly Zimmerli's in the treatment of Isaiah below.[9]

Because the correspondence pattern deals directly with the question of retribution in the Old Testament one cannot altogether avoid the question raised by Klaus Koch in his now famous essay: "Gibt es ein Vergeltungsdogma im Alten Testament?"[10] In an extensive treatment of Old Testament texts Koch argues that there is no doctrine of retribution in the Old Testament. Where it speaks of Yahweh's judgment, that must not be understood as retribution according to prescribed norms. Yahweh does not in this context function as judge. There are no judicial norms or prescribed punishments that determine the judgment. The judgment is not independent of the crime or sin. Rather it is rooted directly in the sin in a relationship of deed and its consequence. The evil that one does comes back upon the sinner even as the good comes upon the righteous. There is a connection between the deed and its results. One may speak of the fate one creates for oneself out of one's actions ("menschlicher Tat entspringendes Schicksal"). One of the clearest ways of conveying this notion is the metaphor of the seed and its fruit (e.g. Hos 8:7; 10:12–13). Some of the technical vocabulary of "retribution" also conveys the *Tun-Ergehen* connection, e.g. *šillēm, pāqad, hēšîb,* and many words can represent both a sin and its punishment (e.g. *ra'*, *'āwōn*). This does not mean for Koch that the process is purely immanental or mechanical. Yahweh is actively involved in the process. He is the one who makes the connection. That is, Yahweh links a deed back to the doer. He sets the deed in power so that the negative fate comes out of the negative deed and vice versa. Yahweh brings back not some strange "punishment" as a result but something indissolubly linked to the deed. He completes the process so that the fate arising from the human deed and the destiny that comes to one from Yahweh are not to be finally separated.

Koch argues his case out of the whole range of Old Testament literature. In the prophets, which are the subject of this study, he confines himself to Hosea but maintains Hosea is only an illustration of what is common to the other prophets. His essay has produced a large amount of response both pro and con and he has gathered some of that response as well as other

[7] J. Fichtner, "Jesaja unter den Weisen," *ThLZ* 74 (1949) 75–80.

[8] W. Zimmerli, "Verkündigung und Sprache der Botschaft Jesajas", *Studien zur Alttestamentlichen Theologie und Prophetie* (München: Kaiser, 1974) 73–87.

[9] M. Lichtenstein has done an excellent brief study of this device as conveyed via the imagery of pits, nets, and traps. See his article, "The Poetry of Poetic Justice: A Comparative Study in Biblical Imagery," *JANES* 5 (1973) 255–65.

[10] K. Koch, "Gibt es ein Vergeltungsdogma im Alten Testament?" *ZThK* 52 (1955) 1–42.

related pieces in an important collection of articles on the whole subject of retribution.[11]

The most recent critical engagement with Koch appears in an article by John Barton on natural law and poetic justice in the Old Testament.[12] Barton properly questions some of the assumptions about Hebrew mentality and language that are present in Koch's arguments. He goes on to say that the correspondence of sin and judgment in the prophets in the sense of a divine poetic justice probably reflects some notion of natural law in prophets "implicitly appealing to a human consensus about what sort of acts are just and unjust . . ."[13] The pervasive character of the phenomenon of poetic justice indicates that Barton may be on the right track in seeing the judgment of God in these cases as derived purely from the revelation of moral norms. But the diverse uses of this pattern in the prophets suggest both that it is rooted as much in universal literary norms as in universal moral norms and that several influences may have brought about the prophetic propensity for poetic justice.

It was not and is not the goal of this study to resolve the much-debated issue of the existence or non-existence of a concept of retribution in the Old Testament. But a number of the texts Koch takes up reflect the correspondence pattern, and other texts under discussion here seem to bear in one way or another on Koch's thesis. Indeed one can not take up the subject of judgment in the Old Testament without dealing in some fashion with the retribution idea. That is even more the case with the passages which point to a correlation between sin and judgment. It is exactly the existence of a relationship that prompts Koch's question and the answer he gives. Some attention, therefore, needs to be given to the question in discussing the passages and the theology of judgment they manifest both individually and in relation to one another even though that is not the primary aim of this investigation.

The heart of the study is the examination of individual passages in prophetic literature—and a few in non-prophetic materials—to see in detail how the correspondence of sin and judgment is manifest and worked out. On that basis a classification can be proposed (though not a rigid one). We shall also seek to discern from the examples what can be suggested about the source and setting of the correspondence pattern before turning to the theology of judgment worked out from the texts considered.

[11] K. Koch, ed. *Um das Prinzip der Vergeltung in Religion und Recht* (Darmstadt: Wissenschaftliche Buchgesellschaft, 1972).

[12] J. Barton, "Natural Law and Poetic Justice in the Old Testament," *JTS* 30 (1979) 1–14.

[13] *Ibid.*, 13.

CHAPTER I

The Correspondence of Sin and Judgment in Prophetic Texts

Hosea

The prophet Hosea provides an appropriate starting point for an examination of the correspondence of sin and punishment in the prophetic tradition. He provides a variety of examples of the ways in which the prophets make such correspondence and thus functions as a kind of paradigm for the phenomena under study. Further, Hosea is the example that Koch uses to demonstrate the *Tun-Ergehen* relationship in the prophets. By means of concrete example and explicit theological statement the prophet bears witness to the appropriate justice of God in his dealings with Israel.

Hosea 2:2–15

The allegory of Israel as the harlotrous wife of Yahweh offers a type of correspondence between sin and punishment that is accomplished through the use of extended metaphor. In other words a metaphor, i.e. the language and imagery of harlotry, is created to depict in a special way the sin of Israel. That metaphor is then prolonged and extended to function also as a vehicle for announcing punishment. Insofar as the metaphor is appropriate for characterizing the sin, the extension of it serves to create a correlation between the sin described in this way and the judgment announced against the sin.

It is unnecessary to deal with every facet of the allegory in order to recognize this metaphorical correlation. The force of the metaphor of the harlotrous wife to describe the sin of Israel is powerful and easy to recognize. Such a metaphor is appropriate in part because of the similarity of the marriage relationship to the covenant relationship. Harlotry as going after lovers outside of and in violation of the relationship of undivided loyalty between husband and wife vividly uncovers the nature of Israel's sin. That sin is further disclosed by the realization of the role of the sexual dimension in the fertility rites of Canaanite ritual and thus the further appropriateness of the imagery of adultery and harlotry as a way of depicting what Israel has done.

In the process of the extended metaphor there appears three times a "therefore" (*lākēn*) followed by an announcement of what Yahweh will do against faithless Israel (vv 8, 11, and 16). Attempts to understand the logical movement of the allegory and the sequence of "therefore" statements have led to various proposals for rearranging the verses. All such proposals create larger problems than they resolve; it is better to assume that various oracles or elements of the Hoseanic tradition have been brought together in a fashion that is not strictly logical in its movement but is clear in its meaning and powerful in its expression.[1]

The "therefore" sections which function as announcements of judgment in response to the indictments of harlotry do not in each case express strict judgment. Nor do they form discrete and separable sections within the larger unit.[2] But in the first two examples announcements of a future judgment, which have elements of both punishment and discipline, are correlated in direct fashion with the preceding accusations. Verse 7 indicts Israel for worshipping the Canaanite deities to secure from them the fertility and rich productivity of the land. That indictment is formulated in the language of the wife going after her lovers because they provide the desired gifts. The punishment is to take away the fertility and productivity Israel desires. But it is expressed in a way appropriate to the metaphor of guilt (vv 8–9). The one who says she will go after other lovers will find her way blocked with thorn-hedges and stone walls so that she cannot find her way or her lovers. Being cut off from what she sees as the source of the gifts, she will find herself in a worse state than before so that her desire will be to return to her husband and the original relationship.

Verse 10 continues the metaphor and makes the same point as in the preceding verses but this time the crime and punishment are made quite explicit and correlated very closely. In addition whereas verses 8–9 subordinated the word of punishment to the note of discipline, verses 10ff. focus upon God's activity in punishing his faithless wife:

Sin: But she does not acknowledge
that it is *I* who gave her
the grain and the wine and the oil . . .

Judgment: Therefore I will take back
my grain at its time
and my wine in its season . . .

The verses that follow elaborate this word of judgment via the harlotry image as Yahweh announces he will strip Israel of all the gifts whose true source she would not acknowledge and expose her shame and nakedness, leaving her without the rich gifts she sought from the Canaanite gods: wool,

[1] See the summary statement of J. L. Mays, *Hosea* (OTL; Philadelphia: Westminster, 1969) 37: "The best explanation of this ambiguity of structure is the assumption that Hosea or a disciple took oracles in which he had employed the same allegory and wove them into this now inseparable fabric to fashion a kerygmatic unity (H. W. Wolff)."

[2] For example, verse 11, which is the *second* "therefore" statement, looks back to verse 10 (grain and wine) but also back to verse 6 (wool and flax), which is prior to the *first* "therefore" statement.

flax, vines, fig trees, and the like. The sin is that Israel will not acknowledge the source of her gifts. The punishment is strictly correlated to the sin: The gifts will be taken away.

A final "therefore" (*lākēn*) comes in v 16. This announcement is tied now to the sins described in verse 15 but it actually grows out of the whole preceding section. The *lākēn*, however, does not in this case introduce words of punishment as one expects but the astonishing words of Yahweh's actions to restore his bride as at the beginning ("the wilderness," "the days of her youth," "the time when she came out of the land of Egypt"). The harlotry image still provides the framework and Yahweh acts as the husband wooing his faithless wife back to him (cf. *m^{e}patteyhā, dibbartî 'al libbāh*).[3] He seduces her, makes love to her, and gives her gifts. The result will be to restore the marriage relationship as it was.

The three "therefore" statements of these verses not only provide a metaphorical correlation of sin and judgment but in their differing character also portray the multi-dimensional character of the Lord's judgment. The judgment serves clearly to punish for sins committed (vv 11ff.). But it also is intended to chasten and correct the harlot people so that they will see the error of their ways and return to Yahweh. Finally Yahweh's actions in response to Israel's sin will bring about a restoration to her former purer state and the relationship with her "husband" as it was at the first and is meant to be continually. The metaphor in its extended character thus serves to portray vividly the sin of Israel and demonstrate how appropriate and unavoidable—in light of the nature of Israel's sin as uncovered by the metaphor—is Yahweh's punishment.[4] It also unifies the various elements of the divine response so that punishment, correction, and restoration are all parts of a whole and integral to the divine judgment. These elements will be found elsewhere in the examples that follow, notably Isa 1:11–16.

Hosea 4:1–3

(1) Hear the word of Yahweh, people of Israel;
  for Yahweh has a controversy with the
    inhabitants of the land,
 because[5] there is no faithfulness, no steadfast love,
  and no knowledge of God in the land.
(2) Cursing and lying and killing
  and stealing and adultery have broken out
    in the land;[6]

[3] See, for example, the extended discussion of the language in Mays, *Hosea*, 44–45.

[4] Ezekiel's even more elaborate use of the harlotry image in chapters 16 and 23 correlates the sin and punishment in similar fashion and will not, therefore, be treated separately.

[5] *kî* here could be either "because" or "that."

[6] LXX has *kechutai epi tēs gēs*, i.e. *pāraṣ bā' āreṣ*. Most commentators restore the *bā'areṣ* to the Hebrew, assuming that the sequence *resh ṣade* in the two words led to the haplography by *homoioteleuton* of *bā' āreṣ*.

(3) Therefore, the land shall dry up,
and all its inhabitants shall languish—
together with the beasts of the field and the birds of the sky;
even the fish of the sea shall be taken away.

These opening verses provide an excellent example of the correlation of sin and punishment centering upon the thematic word *'ereṣ*. "The land" is a central term in Hosea's thought. It belongs to Yahweh and is the locus of his blessing, the means by which he enriches the people. In 2:2 *hā'āreṣ* stands for the people in their sin. Here also "the land" plays a central role both in the description of the sin and in the judgment that will surely follow.

The accusation is given in verses 1 and 2. Verse 1 summons the people and announces Yahweh's lawsuit against them. What is most noticeable in this otherwise straightforward summons is the way the people are addressed. Parallel to "people of Israel" they are called "the inhabitants of the land;" the prophet quite self-consciously seeks to identify them and define them in terms of *the land*. What in another context might be a casual reference to inhabitants of an area, is here a highly intentional parallel to the basic term for this people, *b^e^nê yiśrā'ēl*. Later (v 8) the prophet will use another designation, *'ammî* that also has a particular force to it, but that word would not denote and connote what is important for this judgment speech and is conveyed by *yôš^e^bê hā'āreṣ*.

The description of the sin is given in two lines in 1b–2a, first in terms of sins of omission (*'^e^met, ḥesed*, and *da'at '^e^lōhîm*) and in the second line sins of commission, apparently referring to violation of prohibitions of the Decalogue. In the MT of the first line it is pointedly stated that the qualities required by Yahweh are not present *in the land*. And if the LXX preserves the earlier stage of the Hebrew text, as seems likely, then the locus of sin is reiterated in the list of offences in 2b.

Then in verse 3 appropriately the focus of the punishment corresponds to that of the crime. As the land has been the place of covenant disobedience, now it becomes the place where the curses for disobedience will be invoked. That is described with poetic and theological precision. The picture is of a desolate land and the ending of all life, an image belonging to the curses of Lev 26 and elsewhere.[7] Two other passages depict the land (*'ereṣ*) withering (*'umlal*) and languishing (*'ābal*) as a curse for breaking covenant (Isa 24:4ff.[8] and 33:8–9). The final correlation of the offence and its punishment comes in

[7] See Paul Riemann, *Desert and Return to Desert in the Pre-Exilic Prophets*. Unpublished Ph.D. dissertation, Harvard University, 1964.

[8] Isa 24:1ff. appears to betray the influence of Hosea 4 in several respects, e.g., the repeated reference to *'ereṣ* (vv 1, 2, 3, [2x] 5, 6 [2x]) and its inhabitants (vv 1, 5, and 6), the use and pairing of *'umlal* and *'ābal* (vv 4 and 7), and the phrase *w^e^hāyāh kā'ām kakkohen* (v 2 and Hos 4:9). To the extent that Isa 24 reflects any dependence on Hosea 4 it underscores all the more the covenantal character of 4:1ff. and the imagery of the curses.

the parallelism in 3b of *hāʾāreṣ* and *yôšēb bāh*. The identifying and central phrase *yôšᵉbê hāʾāreṣ* has been broken up into the subjects of the balanced cola of v 3b, i.e. the objects of the punishment: The *land* withers; *its inhabitants* fade away.[9]

By means of repetition, parallelism, and the device of using a stereotyped phrase in the indictment and then breaking it up in the announcement of punishment, Hosea correlates the promised punishment with the sin of Israel and indicates thereby the critical and central place of "the land" in Israel's life and death.[10] The land was the salvation gift par excellence, Yahweh's possession, and the source of Israel's richest blessing. But that gift and that blessing have become now the source and locus of Israel's disobedience and rebellion against Yahweh.[11] The people have sought to gain the blessings of the land from some other power than Yahweh and they have made the land a place where violation of the covenantal commands runs rampant. So the land will become the place of Yahweh's punishment.

Following Koch, Wolff detects in the formulation of this judgment speech evidence of the *Tun-Ergehen* sequence:

> It is noticeable that the judgment results not from the direct actions of Yahweh himself, but from "an organic structure of order," "a sphere in which one's actions have fateful consequences" which Yahweh puts into effect. This conception results from a synthetic view of life.[12]

Such an interpretation of the unit may well be correct but it is difficult to prove conclusively. The punishment is not ascribed to Yahweh's direct actions but that is true of a number of judgment speeches even as many or more ascribe a direct causation to Yahweh. In any particular case one could hardly predict which way the judgment would be described. It may be that the manner of announcing punishment here reflects the synthetic view of life, as Koch and others have sought to describe the *Tun-Ergehen* relationship. Yet one could not preclude the possibility that the formulation of the punishment is not because of a particular structure of order, but rather to underscore the fact that Yahweh will punish when Israel has sinned.

[9] Here is another example of the break-up of stereotyped phrases involving a construct chain. Cf. Y. Avishur, "Pairs of Synonymous Words in the Construct State (and in Appositional Hendiadys) in Biblical Hebrew," *Semitics* 2 (1971–72) 17–81.

[10] On the theme of the land in the Old Testament see Walter Brueggemann, *The Land* (Philadelphia: Fortress, 1977).

[11] "Yahweh's case is brought against people whose responsibility to him lies in the fact of their residence in the land and the history which brought them to its blessing," (Mays, *op. cit.* 62).

[12] Wolff, *Hosea*, 68.

Hosea 4:4–6

(4) Yea, let no one bring complaint,
and no one accuse.
Against you is my complaint, O priest![13]
(5) You shall stumble (*wᵉkāšaltāh*) by day[14]
and the prophet also shall stumble
(*wᵉkāšal*) with you by night.
I will destroy (*wᵉdāmîtî*) your mother[15]
(6) since my people are destroyed (*nidmû*)
for want of the knowledge.[16]
Because you indeed have rejected (*mā'astā*) the knowledge,
I reject you (*wᵉ'em'āsᵉkā*) as my priest,
Because you have forgotten (*wᵉtiškaḥ*) the
instruction of your God,
I in turn[17] will forget (*'eškaḥ*) your sons.

Norbert Lohfink's detailed study of this passage with particular attention to the repetition of verbs and that stylistic device as a way of correlating offence and punishment eliminates the need for further exhaustive analysis. A summary account of the correspondence pattern in these verses in the light of Lohfink's careful work will point up how they provide one of the most extensive illustrations of this rhetorical phenomenon in the prophets.

Most interpreters deal with these verses as part of a larger unit (Mays, vv 4–10; Wolff, vv 4–19; Rudolph, vv 1–10). But they also recognize vv 4–6 as a section within the larger unit, noting a shift from second person singular address to third person in vv 7ff. One can properly treat vv 4–6 and 7–10 as two sub-units continuing the concerns of vv 1–3 (*rîb*, lack of knowledge) but now focused on the priests. The unit and distinctiveness of these three sections (1–3, 4–6, and 7–10) are underscored by the fact that the correspondence motif is clearly present in all three passages and stated as theological principle (v 9) but they are worked out quite differently in each instance.

The passage 4–6 is a complex one with difficult textual, lexical, and syntactical issues. It is built entirely around the repetition of paired words:

[13] Reading *'immᵉkā rîbî* for MT. Some such emendation of the MT, which is incomprehensible in context, is proposed by virtually all commentators.

[14] Reading *wᵉkāšaltāh yôm* for *wᵉkāšaltā hayyôm*.

[15] On the three generation scheme in this passage and elsewhere see N. Lohfink, "Zu Text und Form von Os 4, 4–6," *Biblica* 42 (1961) 308–311.

[16] On this clause as an asyndetic causal clause related to 5b see Lohfink, "Zu Text und Form . . . ," 327; W. Rudolph, *Hosea* (KAT, 13,1; Gerd Mohn: Gutersloher Verlagshaus, 1966) 97 and the references given there.

[17] Note a kind of syntactical inclusio around the two parallel bicola at the end of this unit. An emphasis upon the one doing the sin, the priest, is accomplished by the *kî-'attāh* at the beginning, and an equal and responding emphasis on the one bringing the punishment is given in the concluding *gam-'ānî*.

rîb (4), *kāšal* (5), *dāmāh* (5 and 6), *da'at* (6), *mā'as* (6), *šākaḥ* (6) and *kōhēn* (4 and 6). The verbs in this case, except for the verbal forms of *rîb*, and even they may not be an exception,[18] all serve to relate Yahweh's pending judgment to the present and past sins of the priesthood. But the manifold correspondence is accomplished with a certain amount of variety and complexity unlike such a passage as Isa 33:1 where there is extensive repetition but it is redundant and monotonous albeit quite clear and unmistakable in its intent.

The accusation begins with the bringing of the *rîb* in verse 4. Then in verse 5 the passage moves immediately to announcement of punishment with apparently three cola describing Yahweh's judgment against priest, prophet, and mother of the priest before giving any indication of the reason for this judgment. But in 6a a reason is given that correlates the sin with the punishment just announced. The key word is *dāmāh*, here meaning "destroy".[19] Because the people are *destroyed* for lack of knowledge about God, the teaching of which is the priests' responsibility, Yahweh will *destroy* their mother.[20] Then in 6b and 6c in parallel bicola the correlation of judgment to sin is reiterated. The priest's *rejection* of *hadda'at* means Yahweh will *reject* the priest. He has forgotten Yahweh's *tôrāh*, so Yahweh will forget him. All of the descriptions have to do with the failure of the priestly responsibilities. All of the judgment verbs belong to the vocabulary of Yahweh's negative actions of punishment or abandonment. But by the correspondence of these verbs general words of judgment are correlated precisely to the priestly sin so that the priesthood will know in the judgment what has brought it about. The rhetoric of these words of judgment has this correlation as its primary intention, but as that happens the character of the appropriate judgment becomes clear. The priestly office is taken away and the priestly house and line come under the judgment (cf. 1 Sam 2 and Amos 7:16–17).

The presence of the series of three lines in which the nature of the sin will be the nature of the punishment makes it highly likely that the first of the four sentences of the judgment speech (5ab) also contained at one time a correlation of sin and judgment around the verb *kāšal*. The presence of *nābî'* in 5ab is suspect as far as the original form of the text is concerned inasmuch as there is no further reference to the prophet in this unit while the following verses continue to speak quite specifically about the priest. In addition other references to the prophet in Hosea are positive rather than

[18] If vv 4–6 are to be seen as a response by the prophet to a protest on the part of a priest at the severity of 4:1–3 (so Wolff and Mays), then to some degree *yārēb* represents the continuing offense of the priest and *rîbî* Yahweh's response to that. The text, of course, does not give details at this point.

[19] On *dāmāh III* "destroy" see Walter Baumgartner, *Hebräisches und Aramäisches Lexikon*, 216.

[20] The mother here belongs to a three generation scheme—mother of priest, priest, and sons of priest—indicating complete destruction of the priestly house.

negative in tone. Wilhelm Rudolph has sought to reconstruct the text of 5b as follows:

> *w^e kāšal gam b^e kā ʿammî kallaylāh*
> "since by your fault my people have stumbled as though it were night."

While such a proposal is possible and makes good sense of the text, it involves a much too tortuous reconstruction of the original form of the present *nābîʾ*.[21] It is more likely as Wolff and Lohfink have suggested that *nābîʾ* was a later addition to the text which would have read originally, according to Lohfink: *kāšal gam ʿam kallaylāh*. Like 6a this would have been asyndetically related to the preceding clause and translated: "since my people stumble also as in the night."[22] Any reconstruction of the original text is speculative, but such a proposal is as plausible as any inasmuch as it takes all factors into consideration. Like the other verbs of this passage *kāšal* is used elsewhere as a prophetic judgment motif (Hos 5:5, Isa 3:7, 8:15; 28:13; 31:3; Jer 6:21 etc.) and can also refer to the distress inflicted upon a people (Ps 107:12). This reconstruction also produces a parallel between the two lines 5ab and 5c–6a that is analogous to the parallel character of the two remaining lines in verse 6 noted above. As the final two lines deal with the rejection of the priest because of his rejection of the knowledge and instruction, so the first two lines would deal with the destruction of the priest because of his causing the people to be destroyed. The central term *haddaʿat* then links the two parallel sets together.

The word of the prophet, therefore, announces a judgment against the priesthood which point for point matches the sin it has committed. The heaping up of these verbs underscores heavily the character of the priestly sin and declares an appropriate justice. As they have done, it will be done to them. The talionic emphasis is inescapable in such an extended correspondence as these verses contain. The punishment remains on a general level and points to the general kind of prophecy of destruction common to the prophets. But in this general destruction the priest will be included as an individual and his office and line will come under judgment.

Hosea 4:7–10

> (7) According to their increase in number, thus they
>   sinned against me;
>   I will change their glory into shame.
> (8) They eat (*ʾākal*) the sin of my people;
>   they are greedy for their iniquity.
> (9) It shall be like people, like priest:
>   I will visit upon him his ways;
>   His deeds I will return to him

[21] See Rudolph's discussion (*Hosea*, 97) for details. The *nun* and *beth* are a misreading of the similarly written *beth* and *kaph*. The *yodh* of *nbyʾ* was originally attached to *ʿam*.

[22] Lohfink, "Zu Text und Form . . . ," 330–31.

(10) They shall eat (*'ākal*) and not be satisfied.
They have played the harlot, but shall not increase.
For they have abandoned Yahweh to cherish (11) harlotry.

The correspondence pattern continues in this announcement of judgment against the priest(s). It appears in two forms. Verse 9 expresses the correspondence in terms of a general principle. This statement, along with similar general formulations of the correlation of sin and punishment, is discussed in the final chapter. The second form of correspondence centers upon the repetition of the verb *'ākal* and works out the punishment in terms of the frustration of the intended result of the crime. The priests "eat" or "consume" the sin of the people. The precise meaning of this idea is not altogether clear, but it is likely that it has reference to the priestly right to eat part of the sacrifices. The more sacrifices for sin the greater the priestly revenues. They encourage the sacrifices and partake of them when in fact the whole sacrificial apparatus has become sin in the sight of Yahweh because it has become a device to manipulate the deity and cover over disobedience of covenant (see 5:6; 6:6; 8:11, 13). So the sin of the priests is in their encouraging and eating the sinful sacrifices.

But the divine judgment is appropriate to the form of the sin and indeed takes place in the very act of the sin. In the style of the "futility curses" the prophet announces a punishment that consists of frustrating the intention of the sin. The priests will eat but not be satisfied. The "eating" that is sinful leads only to hunger. The prophet does not spell out the context of such a judgment. It may be that he has in mind a time when the decimation of people and land is so great that the priestly portions of sacrifice are not enough to still the gnawing pangs of hunger. The concise form of the judgment speech, however, allows one only to speculate at this point.

The frustration of the sin as a form of judgment is expressed a second time in the parallel colon. The harlotry that takes place in the cult—whether by priest or people—and is designed to bring increase and profit—whether to priest or people[23] —will not achieve that result.

Hosea 7:11–12

(11) Ephraim has become like a dove,
easily fooled, lacking sense.
They have called to Egypt,
gone to Assyria.
(12) As they go I will spread
my net over them.
Like a bird of the sky I will bring them down;

[23] It is a debatable point as to whether this sentence has in mind profits acquired by the priests as they tempt the people into consorting with sacred prostitutes (so Rudolph) or the increase in fertility for land and people as a goal of the priests' own participation in the *hieros gamos* (so Mays).

I will chastise[24] them according to the
report of their evil.[25]

These verses fall within a larger series, the limits of which are differently defined. They are in themselves clearly a whole judgment speech within the series. Verse 10 belongs to a preceding unit about Ephraim as it speaks of Yahweh in the third person; verse 13 has an introductory *'ôy* indicating a new unit in the series.

The correspondence style is clear and explicit though in this case it depends entirely on figures of speech, metaphor, and simile. Ephraim is indicted for or accused of being a foolish, silly dove in turning to Egypt and Assyria. As in the case of Judah and Isaiah's prophecy, so the northern kingdom in turning to foreign powers for help betrays her abandonment of Yahweh. Her sin in this case, however, is also stupidity and folly. Failing to keep herself dependent on Yahweh rather than the military strength of other nations is stupid politics as well as bad faith, according to the prophetic word.

So even as Israel plays the fowl, then Yahweh will play the fowler. The imagery of the indictment carries over into the announcement of judgment. It is one of the common images of judgment and conquest, appearing numerous times in the Old Testament and in ancient Near Eastern art—the net as a means of conquering one's enemies (see, for example, the Stele of Vultures). The Mari letters give several instances where Dagan through his "prophetic" messengers (*āpilum* and *gamatum*) gives a word of judgment in which the god announces he will gather up the offender in a net.[26] The imagery of Yahweh casting (*pāraś*) his net in judgment appears elsewhere in the Old Testament prophets, e.g. Ezek 12:13; 17:20; 32:3. The last instance, which is not being considered separately here, may be brought into relationship with Hos 7:11–12 because it also expresses indictment and announcement of judgment with the same kind of imagery, the Egyptian pharaoh being compared to a dragon troubling and fouling the waters who will be caught in Yahweh's net. The oracle in this case, however, goes on to express the judgment of destruction in much more extended and different images.

[24] Vocalizing *'ayassᵉrēm*.

[25] Reading *lᵉrā'ātām* for *la'adātām*.

[26] ARMT X. 80.11.14–15; XIII 23, 11. 9–10. Cf. G. Dossin, "Une révélation du dieu Dagan à Terqa," *RA* 42 (1948) 128–32. The example in ARMT X is particularly interesting in this connection because of the possibility that it represents an instance of poetic justice in which a person's acts become the means or context for his or her downfall. The text reads *ana šetim ša uqaṣṣaru*. Lichtenstein, *op. cit.*, following W. Romer, translates *ša uqaṣṣaru*. "which he is fabricating," i.e. "I will gather him into the net which he is fabricating," an excellent example of the trap that one sets becoming an instrument of one's destruction. Unfortunately, it is not completely certain that *ša uqaṣṣaru* is to be translated in such a way. Alternative translations have been suggested, e.g. "which holds fast" or "which I draw tight" (both translations are proposed by William Moran, "New Evidence from Mari on the History of Prophecy," *Biblica* 50 [1969] 52–53, or "with which I will surround [him]" [CAD] 8, 262).

What is particularly interesting in the style of Hos 7:11–12 is that the imagery of the stupid bird flying foolishly to Assyria allows or even calls for the use of a strong and not uncommon metaphor of judgment—Yahweh spreading his net to catch his enemies like birds. The correspondence may go even further than is immediately apparent when one considers that only once in the prophets is the term *rešet*, "net" used to refer to the sin of the people. That is two chapters earlier in Hos 5:1: "You have been a snare for Mizpah, a net cast upon Tabor." Now Yahweh becomes a net or spreads a net over Israel. The imagery which previously denoted Israel's sin in chapter 7 becomes the imagery for Yahweh's judgment.

If the emendation proposed above—which is commonly assumed on the basis of LXX *tēs thlipseōs autōn*—for the end of v 12 is correct, then the correspondence between the judgment and the sin is even further emphasized. It explicitly compares with or is carried out according to the report of their wickedness.

While we are dealing with two separate figures of speech, the simile of the dove and the metaphor of the fowler, one notes the appropriateness of the correspondence effected for expressing the notion of divine judgment. The key clause in this regard is the beginning of verse 12, *ka'ᵃšer yēlēkû*, "as they go" referring back to *'aššûr hālākû* of verse 11, "they go to Assyria." In all this maneuvering back and forth between Assyria and Egypt, which is both stupid and desertion of Yahweh, they will be caught and doomed just like a bird in the fowler's net. That, of course, is just what happened. The pendulum swing of Israel between Assyria and Egypt in the third quarter of the eighth century led to her downfall (see 2 Kgs 15–17). That downfall resulting from her foolish policies was, according to the prophet, Yahweh's net.

Hosea 8:1–6

(1) To your mouth, the trumpet!
    One like the eagle is over Yahweh's house,
  Because they have broken my covenant,
    and against my instruction they have rebelled.
(2) To me they cry out:
    My God, we Israel know you.
(3) Israel has rejected (*zānaḥ*) the good;
    an enemy shall pursue him.
(4) They themselves made kings, but not through me.
    They set up princes, but I did not authorize it.
  With their silver and gold they made for themselves idols
    so that it might be cut off.
(5) Your bull is rejected (*znḥ*), O Samaria;
    my anger burns against them.
  How long will they be incapable of innocence?
(6)   for what has Israel to do with it?[27]

[27] On this difficult colon see the discussion in Rudolph, *Hosea*, 158.

An artisan made it.
It is not a god.
Yea, splinters (?) shall become
Samaria's bull.

The correspondence of sin and judgment in this passage revolves around the repetition of the verb *zānaḥ*. Unfortunately the form of the verb in verse 5 is disputed. MT has a third person perfect, i.e. "he has rejected," which does not agree with the first person divine speech of the parallel colon or the preceding verse.[28] BH[3] and BHS propose to read first person *zānaḥtî*, which would fit the context but lacks any basis in terms of the textual evidence. Wolff proposes to read an imperative *zinḥî* while Mays vocalizes the form as a passive participle *zānūaḥ*. Both of these forms have some support in the versions. Rudolph apparently would read *znḥ* as an infinitive absolute and translate as a passive. Some sort of passive translation seems most likely in the context. An imperative reading is possible but the parallel colon and the general character of the unit make that less likely than the passive. The second colon of verse 5 announces Yahweh's anger against Israel. The first colon should match that expression.

While it is not possible to reach a conclusive resolution of the problem of *znḥ* in verse 5, the prophetic propensity for the stylistic device of using a key verb characterizing the sin to describe the judgment tends to support the passive interpretation. Israel's sin is summarized in verse 3 as a rejection of the "good," a term that can refer both to Yahweh (see Amos 5:14–15) and to the requirements of the relationship between Yahweh and Israel. The content of this rejection of the good lies very much in Israel's idolatry. So it is that the announcement of judgment reverses the situation and focuses attention rhetorically on both the sin and the means by which it was accomplished. As Israel by her idols has rejected Yahweh, so now Yahweh will reject her idol and kindle his anger against the people. The focus of the sin becomes the focus of the judgment, and the character of both actions is the same—rejection.

This correspondence of sin and punishment is then carried on in the imagery of sowing and reaping in verse 7, on which see the last chapter.

Hosea 10:1–2

(1) Israel is a flourishing vine.
that bears fruit on it.
As his fruit increased (*rôb*)
so he increased (*hirbāh*) altars (*mizbeḥôt*).
As his land made good (*ṭôb*)
they made good (*hêṭîbû*) pillars (*maṣṣēbôt*).

[28] It should be noted, however, that Israel is addressed in the first colon and referred to in the third person in the second colon. The incompatibility of persons is, therefore, already and inextricably in the line.

(2) Their heart is tricky;
now they shall bear their guilt.
He himself will break their altars (*mizbeḥôtām*)
and destroy their pillars (*maṣṣēbôtām*).[29]

The indictment is carried by imagery and word play. It recalls the fruitfulness of Israel in the land. But then the prophet points to a direct connection between the increase of the land and the increase of *maṣṣēbôt* and *mizb*^e^*ḥôt*, which are implements of a slippery, tricky heart.[30] Increase of wealth was associated with cultic celebration and the implements of Canaanite worship (*maṣṣēbāh*). Israel succumbed to a thoroughly Canaanite notion of the cult, that its function was to ensure fertility of the land and its produce. This is expressed by the wordplay indicated in both the Hebrew and the English of the above translation.[31] The operative terms in the indictment are *mizb*^e^*ḥôt* and *maṣṣēbôt*. These are the manifestations of Israel's sin; they are also the basis for the correspondence between sin and judgment. The announcement of punishment in 2b (signalled by the *ʿattāh*—see 5:7; 8:10, 13 where *ʿattāh* also signals the punishment) is concise and to the point. The instruments and manifestations of their sin become the focus of Yahweh's judgment. He will tear down their *mizb*^e^*ḥôt* and destroy their *maṣṣēbôt*. The irony in this correspondence of crime and punishment is recognized by Mays who says: "The altars and pillars will in the end serve as a place of knowing Yahweh's nearness—when they are shattered and destroyed!"[32] Thus by wordplay as well as repetition of the key nouns the prophet creates a correspondence that illumines the inner relationship between human offense and the divine response of justice. In the judgment that is soon to come upon the nation those devices through which Israel was false to Yahweh will be destroyed by him.

Hosea 10:13b–15

(13b)[33] Because you have trusted in your chariots,[34]
in the number of your warriors,
(14) a clamor shall arise against your people,
and all your fortresses shall be destroyed,
as Shalman destroyed Bet-arbel

[29] The translation here follows closely that of Mays, *Hosea*, 137.

[30] It is possible that the verb *ḥālaq* comes from *ḥālaq* I = "divide," but one would expect the vocalization *ḥullaq*.

[31] Note further that the poetry also includes very careful rhyming elements across the two lines of 1b and 1c:
k^e^*rōb l*^e^*piryô* rhymes with *k*^e^*ṭôb l*^e^*'arṣô*;
hirbah lammizb^e^*ḥôt* rhymes with *hêṭîbû maṣṣēbôt*.

[32] Mays, *Hosea*, 139.

[33] On v 13a see the final chapter.

[34] Reading *b*^e^*rikb*^e^*kā* with LXX^A^ for MT *b*^e^*dark*^e^*kā*. It is, of course, possible that the MT is correct. If so, it would not significantly alter the point being made.

when in the day of battle
    mother was dashed over children.
(15) So it shall be done[35] to you, house of Israel
    because of your greatest evil.
In the dawn the king of Israel
    shall surely be cut off.

The sin of Israel in this passage is comparable to Judah's temptation and failure in Isaiah's time—trusting in military might—chariots (?) and warriors. It is the failure to follow the rules of holy war in Israel, the basic requirement of which is faith in Yahweh.

In verses 14–15 the announcement of punishment is given in this judgment oracle. As Israel's sin is to put her trust in the weapons of war, so her punishment will be destruction by those same weapons. "A clamor (*šāʾôn*) shall arise among your people." The *šāʾôn* is usually the din or tumult of battle and war. "Your people" may be a reference to the army itself (cf. Num 20:20; 21:33; Josh 8:3, etc.).[36] The rest of verse 14 describes a previous terrible event of war and says that is what will happen to Israel. Verse 15 refers to the destruction or death of the king in the early dawn. *Bᵉšaḥar* is often changed to *bᵉśaʿar* ("in the storm"—see RSV), but this misses the point. The king is leader of the armies in which Israel trusts. The reference to dawn has in mind the time of battle. There are several references to battle taking place at dawn (Josh 6:15) or in the early morning (Josh 8:10, 10:9; 1 Sam 11:11; 2 Kgs 3:22; 6:15). The battle order—attack at dawn!—is a familiar command which points to the frequent military strategy of going into battle in the early morning light.

The passage announces, therefore, that because of Israel's evil, the violation of the tenets of holy war by failing to trust in Yahweh and depending instead on their own military power, Yahweh will now bring *his* war on them. The correspondence of sin and punishment is conceptual and does not depend on stylistic devices of repetition and figures of speech. Once again, however, the instruments and manifestation of Israel's sin will be the focus or instrument of her punishment.

The punishment announced is realistic. It is not capricious or irrational because it corresponds to the sin. Indeed the history of Israel's latter years confirms both Hosea's description of the sin and his description of the judgment if one does not read too literally the word about the death of the king. One observes also here the consequential relationship between the deed (sin) and its result (punishment). The latter will grow out of the former. In fact the oracle does not even stress in any fashion the controlling action of Yahweh in the destruction, though that may be assumed.

[35] Reading *yēʿāśeh* for MT *ʿāśāh*. See discussion in Mays and Rudolph.

[36] Mays, *Hosea*, 149.

Amos

Amos 5:7, 10–11

(7) (Woe)[1] the ones turning justice to wormwood,
    and casting the righteousness to the earth!
(10) They hate the advocate in the gate;
    the one speaking truthfully they abhor.
(11) Therefore, because you trample on the poor,
    and you take exactions of grain from him,
houses of hewn stone you have built,
    but you shall not dwell in them;
pleasant vineyards you have planted
    but you shall not drink their wine.

The analysis of these verses as a unit into which verses 8–9 have been inserted is generally though not universally assumed and convincingly argued by J. L. Mays.[2] The three verses comprise a judgment speech arising out of a woe saying that identifies those to whom the speech is directed and characterizes their sin. That characterization in the opening verse is a general indictment for those who discard justice and righteousness and turn them into injustice and unrighteousness. That indictment continues in verses 10–11a and becomes increasingly concrete. It involves the maladministration of justice, the use of the courts legally or illegally to oppress the poor and build an accumulation of wealth off the backs of the poor. The judicial and economic spheres, which are all too intimately related, are the focus of attack because they have been twisted into something utterly different than intended in the Yahwistic covenant.

The third person indictment shifts to second person in 11b as the prophet focuses directly on the accused ones. That intensity of attack continues in the announcement of punishment, which provides a classic case of the correspondence between sin and judgment where the punishment involves a frustration of the result of the crime. The punishment does not stand outside the sphere of the sinful activity or unconnected to it. It is not inherent in the deed but appropriate to it. That appropriateness is seen in the relationship of intention or result to the punishment. The unjust will not achieve what they

[1] Assuming an original sequence *hwyhhpkym*. The series of *he*'s led to haplography. Even if the *hôy* should not be assumed in the original, the verse is to be understood as a woe-saying comparable to those in Amos 6:1ff.

[2] Mays, *Amos* (OTL; Philadelphia: Westminster, 1969) 90ff.

hope to achieve and that is their punishment. In one sense nothing is said explicitly about what will happen to them. That is all implicit. In light of the larger context one may assume the prophet envisions a fate of destruction or exile or both. Either the elegant homes and vineyards built out of the wealth acquired from the poor will be destroyed or the people themselves will fall by the sword or be carried into exile. There is the actual fate of the oppressors of the poor. But in this case when the prophet announces judgment he says nothing about such things (though elsewhere he does so quite straightforwardly). His intention is to point to the nature of the sin on the one hand, underscoring its character and the intent behind it, and on the other hand to announce a divine justice directed toward this specific crime. While the connection between crime and punishment is neither inherent nor inevitable, it is most real and the prophet chooses to focus upon that and draw attention to it rather than spell out details of the wicked's fate (as he does elsewhere) so that when the judgment comes, those who experience it and those who view it will know quite clearly why these things have happened. The judgment for this particular crime—the economic exploitation of the poor and the use of the system of justice in the process—will not come in some *deus ex machina* fashion. It will happen in the context of the larger stream of the history of this people and God's way with them. But within that stream will come judgment, which through the prophetic word is seen to be a judgment for and appropriate to the sin of the wealthy who trample on the poor.

This particular form of judgment announcement serves also to place the words of sin and judgment in a larger and quite specific context. The announcement of judgment serves to invoke the curses of the covenant as punishment for violation of the covenant. Verse 11 is an example of the "futility curses" known from the first millennium treaties and the lists of curses in Leviticus and Deuteronomy. Indeed both the items mentioned in Amos 5:11 are listed as curses in Deut 28:30 (houses and vineyards) and 39 (vineyards). The announcement of punishment by Amos is almost identical to these curses and one can hardly avoid assuming that the prophet is intentionally calling down the curses of the covenant. At the same time these curses are peculiarly appropriate to the sin and that appropriateness is sharpened by the one modification the prophet makes in each line of v 11:

Deut 28:30	*bayit tibneh* w^{e}*lō’ tēšēb bô*
Amos 5:11b	*bātê gāzît* b^{e}*nîtem* w^{e}*lō’ tēš*^{e}*bû bām*
Deut 28:39	k^{e}*rāmim tiṭṭa‘ . . .* w^{e}*yayin lō’ tišteh*
Amos 5:11b	*karmê ḥemed* n^{e}*ṭa‘tem* w^{e}*lō’ tištû ’et yênām*

The houses are elegant, expensive homes of the wealthy. The vineyards are magnificent. In other words, by the addition to the curse of one word in each line the prophet has achieved a correlation of sin and punishment that would not have been present if the curse formula had been borrowed untouched. The appropriateness of the punishment is made clear: The wealthy who extract their wealth from the poor by oppressing them will be punished by being deprived of the enjoyment of their ill-gotten wealth.

Amos 6:1–7

It is not necessary to examine this judgment speech in detail. The ironic correspondence between sin and punishment has often been noted, and the passage exemplifies the way in which Amos blends sarcasm, irony, rhetorical questions, and other rhetorical elements to convey his message with clarity and force. The initial woe saying is filled with sarcasm, not least of all in Amos's characterization of those he denounces as "the notable ones of the first (*rē'šît*) of the nations." This is intended to represent their own self-evaluation. Hammershaimb has aptly interpreted the expression as meaning "the most prominent men from the best of peoples" (96). They are the elite of Israelite society, a position they assume for themselves or about themselves because of their wealth acquired in violent ways, as the immediate and larger context indicates, and expended in extravagant luxuries. These are, in their opinion, the first and best. All others must come to them. As a result of their ill-gotten wealth and position, they feel totally at ease and secure.

But judgment will come to those who grow fat and wealthy off the backs of others, legally and illegally. So the prophet moves from the indictment which is spelled out at length in vv 1–6 to the succinct announcement of judgment (verse 7 -*lākēn ʿattāh* . . .). By means of irony and word-play the prophet correlates the punishment to the sin. Those whose sin is a self-satisfied claim to be first of all—and by means of violence and injustice—will be given first position as their punishment. But whereas their sin was thinking themselves *rē'šît haggôyīm*, their punishment is to be *b*ᵉ*rôš gōlîm*. The correspondence is both in the double use of *rôš* and its derivatives and in the word-play between *gôyīm* and *gōlîm*. Their security is shattered, and from assuming to be and making themselves first of the people (*gôyīm*) they will become instead first of the exiles (*gōlîm*). Those to whom the people came will, as punishment, lead them into exile.

The correlation between language characterizing sin and that characterizing judgment is carried through at two other points on a lesser level. Not only do those accused see themselves as *rē'šît* but they anoint themselves with the best (*rē'šît*) of oils. Further, the indictment describes the revelry of "those who stretch themselves" (*s*ᵉ*rûḥîm*), and the announcement declares that the revelry of "those who stretch themselves (*s*ᵉ*rûḥîm*) shall pass away (*sār*)." The divine origin of this punishment is not stated but it may be assumed both from the following verse 8 and from other Amos oracles.

Amos 7:16–17

(16) Now, therefore, hear the word of the Lord:
You say, "Do not prophecy against Israel,
do not preach against the house of Isaac."

(17) Therefore thus says the Lord:
"Your wife shall commit harlotry in the city;
your sons and daughters shall fall by the sword;
and your land shall be parcelled out by line.
You yourself shall die in an unclean land;
and Israel shall surely go into exile away from
its land."

This passage in its context is similar in various ways to some of the judgment speeches of the ninth century prophets in 1 and 2 Kings (see below). It is directed toward an individual, an official leader of the kingdom, who has abused his office. It occurs in the context of a narrative that tells of the sin of the accused (though in this case the text does not go on to spell out in narrative the way in which the announcement of punishment is fulfilled).[3]

The correlation of sin and punishment is not achieved in the frequent and more obvious way of repeated words in the indictment and the announcement. Indeed the relationship is not explicit at all. But it is direct and provides an example of that correspondence which appears elsewhere, wherein the punishment is related to the person or, more importantly, to the office, misuse of which has been the heart of the crime.

Verses 10–15 tell of Amaziah's effort as chief priest of the kingdom to stop the prophetic activity of Amos in the northern kingdom. He regards Amos's words as incendiary, if not seditious, and orders him to flee (implying threat?) to Judah and do his prophesying there. It is clear that Amaziah's words are an effort to assert and act by his authority as chief priest of the kingdom. And Amos's response with reference to his call is the counterclaim of another authority as the basis for his actions and words. Indeed the whole account of 7:10–17 revolves around the question of authority and two different ways of viewing the reality in the northern kingdom. One voice and one perspective is that of the prophet as the representative of the divine government; the other is that of the priest, ostensible mediator between Yahweh and the people but here functioning as representative of the human government seeking by his authority as priest to Yahweh to oppose and stop the word of Yahweh as proclaimed by the prophet. Such a use of his priestly office is an utter violation of that office, and the prophet announces (v 17) the judgment that will come for Amaziah's priestly sin summarized succinctly in v 16. The one who misuses the priestly office will lose that office and everything associated with it.

Once again the word of judgment announces a future event of death, destruction, exile, and shame. That event is the pending downfall of the northern kingdom (17c). Amaziah receives no special separate or sudden punishment. His fate is to undergo the fate of others in his kingdom. But the prophet's word serves to draw a connection between crime and punishment,

[3] On these judgment speeches against individuals see Westermann, *Basic Forms of Prophetic Speech* (Philadelphia: Westminster, 1967) 129–68.

to announce that the punishment will in Amaziah's case be peculiarly appropriate to his sin. Each item of the announcement of judgment up to the last expresses a common experience of judgment and can even be related to common treaty curses: becoming a harlot (treaty of Ashurnirari V)[4] , children killed (Vassal Treaties of Esarhaddon; see *ANET*, 539–40, para. 67, 69, 70, 82, 83, 84, etc.), possessions and land divided up (Esarhaddon, *ANET*, 538, para. 42), exile (Deut 28:26, 63ff.). Even the sequence of evil things against wives/women, sons, and daughters is common in the curses. But each one also in a different way strikes at the priestly role and character that has been misused and thus forfeited. The crucial indicator is the announcement of the priest's future death in an *unclean* land. But the priest's holiness and purity are also violated by the harlotry of his wife. And the priestly line as well as the priestly allotment of land will be lost.

The prophet has announced Yahweh's appropriate punishment for the unfaithful priest. By uncovering a particularity hidden in the general fate of the people Yahweh's agent uncovers the true sin of Amaziah and emphasizes that his fate is not merely a matter of being caught up in the larger catastrophe but is indeed a punishment for a quite specific sin.

[4] See discussion in Delbert Hillers, *Treaty Curses and the Old Testament Prophets* (Biblica et Orientalia; Rome: Pontifical Biblical Institute, 1964) 58.

Micah

The eighth century Judean prophet Micah, like his contemporary Isaiah, used the pattern of correspondence between sin and judgment with some frequency and a good deal of diversity. The examples found here range from straight repetition of words to metaphor, word-play, and the correspondence of ideas. Not all of the instances discussed here come necessarily from the prophet himself, and no distinction is being made between Micah and non-Micah material; nevertheless all but one of the examples come from the first three chapters, which are those chapters that are most clearly Micah material. The examples in chapters 2 and 3 undoubtedly belong to the prophet himself.

Micah 1:7

> All her images shall be beaten to pieces,
> all her hires (*'etnanneyhā*) burned in a fire,
> and all her idols I will lay waste.
> For from the hire of a harlot (*'etnān*) she gathered them,
> and to a harlot's hire they shall return.

This verse occurs in the midst of the opening lawsuit which Micah proclaims against Judah and Israel. It is an attack on the idolatry of Samaria as it presently stands in the text and is probably redactional expansion. The precise historical circumstances that brought forth the judgment are not necessary to discern the correspondence between sin and judgment in the passage. It hinges on the three-fold use of *'etnān* "(harlot's) hire." The term is used to characterize the sin of the people but also in this case (unlike Hos 9:1 and Ezek 16) their punishment. Each usage of the term appears to have a slightly different nuance, the last instance being the least clear as far as meaning is concerned.

In the first appearance in verse 7a the word appears in the plural in a sentence stating that her *'etnānîm* will be burned in a fire. This sentence is between two parallel sentences referring to destruction of Israel's images or idols. The parallelism incontrovertibly points to a meaning of *'etnān* in this context that is similar to idol or image. The word is clearly a strange parallel to *pesel* and *'āṣāb*, which fact led older commentators, e.g. Wellhausen, Nowack, Marti, and Smith, and more recently Mays, to alter the text—sometimes quite ingeniously—to find a more acceptable parallel term, even if that involved positing a new root. But the text may be understood as it stands. Eliminating *'etnān* from the text, as has been proposed, eliminates the important word-play that is self evident from the rest of the verse. The parallelism tells us clearly that *'etnān* in this plural usage refers to idols. It is used here because the prophet is going to play on it in the next line of the verse.

There the term *'etnān* has the clear meaning that it has in other contexts—the hire of a harlot. The term used previously to describe the instrument of Israel's sinfulness is now used metaphorically to characterize the manner of her acquiring these images and thus the nature of her sin. They come from hiring herself out as a harlot. That is, Israel has given herself to the worship of other gods and built altars and images out of her prosperity.

The conclusion of the words of judgment then comes in the final colon of verse 7, again in terms of the *'etnān*. The prophet announces that what has been collected from the harlot's hire will return to it. The precise nuance is not entirely clear, but whereas the first use of *'etnān* referred to the idols and the second use to Israel's worship of the foreign gods, this final use seems to point to her subjection to the nations of the foreign gods and the fact that her idols and images will go over to the victorious gods of the other nations. Or if the *'etnān* has in mind the payment to cult prostitutes, then the final usage could refer to the fact that the idols of precious metals and the like would be taken away by others and used in their temples as *'etnān* for temple prostitutes.[1]

The *'etnān* theme thus becomes the center-piece and thematic device of this announcement of judgment, conveying in one word the instrument, character, and punishment of her sin. One is led rather obviously to compare the verse with the long metaphors or allegories of Israel's harlotry in Hos 2 and Ezek 16 and 23.

The judgment appears to be an event of war and destruction, presumably at the hands of a foreign nation. But the only clue to that in these opening verses is the *'etnān* punishment in 7b. The picture is thoroughly one of the theophany or epiphany of the divine warrior who comes from his abode to destroy the sinful city. It is possible to see in 7b the notion that Samaria's deeds effect consequences which become by Yahweh's decision a judgment upon her. That cannot be ruled out as implicit in the correspondence played out here. Neither, however, can one say conclusively that such a notion is intended by the correspondence or to be discerned in it. The fact

[1] "In the only other uses of *'etnān* beyond this text and Hosea, the term is applied to political (Ezek 16:31ff.) and economic relations (Isa 23:17f.) as a characterization of gifts or profits. Perhaps what is meant in v 7b is that the idols have been acquired and established in securing relations with other nations and will be broken up and carried away by one" (Mays, *Micah* [OTL; Philadlephia: Westminster, 1976] 48).

that the final usage of *'etnān zônāh* is unclear accentuates that uncertainty. The *'etnān* references serve primarily to highlight the problem. The primary fact about the judgment is not that it is inherent in and inevitable out of the deed—though that may well be so—but that Yahweh comes to bring it because he finds *'etnān* in his people.

Micah 2:1–5

(1) Woe, those who devise wickedness,
the ones who work at evil on their beds!
In the morning light they do it
because it is in their power.
(2) They covet fields and seize them;
houses, and take them away.
They oppress a man and his house,
a man and his inheritance.
(3) Therefore, thus says the Lord:
I am devising evil against this family,
from which you shall not remove your necks;
nor shall you walk haughtily
for it is an evil time.
(4) In that day a taunt-song shall be raised over you,
a lament shall be sung saying: [omitting *nhyh* as dittogr.]
"We are utterly ruined.
The property of my people is measured: [*yimmad*—cf. LXX]
There is none to return it again: [w^{e}*'ēn mēšîb* l^{e}*šôbēb*—cf. LXX]
Our fields are divided up."[2] [pual for Piel—cf. LXX]
(5) Therefore you shall have none to
cast the line by lot
in the assembly of the Lord.

The indictment in these verses is similar to that in Isa 5:8–10 and the two passages are often paired together as primary witnesses to the disintegration of traditional Yahwistic understanding of the land and the land-grabbing exploits of the rich. They also share in common the correlation of sin and punishment although they work that out in somewhat different fashion (see below on Isa 5:8–10). The unit is a typical judgment speech that begins the indictment with a woe-saying (v 1) characterizing the ones to whom it is addressed, elaborates the accusation in more detail (v 2), then announces the punishment, preceding it with *lākēn kōh 'āmar yhwh* (cf. Isa 5:8–10; Amos 5:7, 10–11; 6:1–7; etc.). The passage contains elements that suggest it has been expanded for a later time.[3] The text is not without its problems, particularly in verse 4, but they do not materially affect the matter under consideration.

[2] The translation of v 4 is taken from Mays, *Micah*, 60f. See his textual notes.

[3] On the literary analysis of this passage see Mays, *Micah*, 60f.

The correspondence between sin and punishment is a major element in the passage and is set forth at the beginning of the announcement of punishment.

> "Woe to the ones devising/planning (*ḥōšᵉbê*) wickedness
> the ones working evil (*ra'*) on their beds."

The key terms are *ḥōšᵉbê* and *ra'*. They are picked up in the opening colon of the announcement of punishment in verse 3:

> *hinᵉnî ḥōšēb 'al-hammišpāḥāh hazzôt rā'āh.*

To those planning *ra'* (wickedness), Yahweh announces that he is planning *rā'āh* (evil, disaster). Their scheme of evil against others will be met by his scheme of evil against them. In the formulation of this correspondence the prophet combines the two parallel cola of the indictment into one, drawing the verb from the first colon, the object from the second. The term *rā'(āh)* is more appropriate not only because it serves rhetorically to combine the cola of the indictment but also because it is especially the term that expresses fully both the negative, wicked actions of human beings and the negative, punishing response of the Lord. The correspondence of human *ra'* and divine *ra'* is, as we shall see, relatively frequent, particularly in Jeremiah, and functions as a kind of general category which specific instances of correlation of sin and punishment particularize. In this case the particularity is in the schemes and secret, internal devising of evil. One notes further that the correlation of human *ra'* and divine *ra'* is further emphasized in verse 3e by the expression: "For it is a time of evil (*rā'āh*)." The reference has in mind the time of judgment referring back to the *rā'āh* of Yahweh at the beginning of the verse (cf. Amos 5:13). But in this context the sentence has a certain ambiguity to it, i.e. because it is a time of wickedness (*ra'*) there will be a time of evil or disaster (*rā'āh*).

The correlation of sin and judgment continues further in the passage and is worked out in terms of the result of the sin of scheming or planning wickedness. In other words the effect of Yahweh's scheme will be the same as the effects of their nocturnal schemes. Those whose sin was the greedy and oppressive seizing of houses and fields belonging to others will be punished by having their own fields portioned out among others. The correspondence catchword is "fields"—*śādôt* (v 2) and *śādênû* (v 4). Micah probably envisioned a redistribution of the lands of the oppressors among the general population. The present form of the text and the context seem to represent an understanding of the punishment in terms of the fall of Judah and Jerusalem though one cannot tell for certain what is envisaged, especially in light of the condition of verse 4. One gets a glimpse of what the judgment will be, and that is confirmed by its correlation with the sin, but how it happens remains much in the dark. What is clear is that the judgment is wrought by God and is like the sin. It is not pictured as a consequence of the sin except by Yahweh's decision to punish the wicked deeds. The judgment corresponds to the sin but becomes a consequence of it only as Yahweh determines that. The text does not go beyond that in describing the inner relation of sin and punishment.

In sum, the prophet directs a judgment speech against elements in Judean society. By correlating the indictment and the announcement of judgment through repetition of action words and other catchwords as well as through an identity of results, the speech underscores with vigor and sharpness the double sin of wicked scheming and its oppressive effects.

Micah 3:1–4

(1) And I said:
Listen, you heads of Jacob
and rulers of the house of Israel!
Is it not for you to know justice?
(2a) haters of good and lovers of evil,
(3) who eat the flesh of my people,
and flay their skin from off them,
and break their bones in pieces
and chop them up like meat[4] in a kettle,
like flesh in a caldron.
(2b) The skin will be torn off them,
their flesh off their bones.
(4) Then they will cry out to the Lord;
but he will not answer them.
He will hide his face from them in that time
because they have made their deeds evil.

This passage offers a quite precise and detailed example of the correspondence of sin and punishment if the literary and textual proposals set forth earlier by Johannes Lindblom[5] and followed most recently by Mays are correct, and they are both possible and plausible. It has long been recognized that v 2b does not make sense in the context for two reasons: (a) it says almost exactly the same thing as 3a with almost the same words; (b) even more importantly, the third person plural suffixes on *'ôrām*, *mē'ᵃlêhem*, *šᵉ'ārām*, and *'aṣmôtām* lack any antecedent and do not fit the second person address of verses 1–2a. Most interpreters regard 2b as an interpolation of some sort (so Nowack, Wellhausen, Robinson, etc.). Some read it as a redactional gloss, but Mays has demonstrated that the redactional work on Micah is far too careful to assume that. With Lindblom he proposes instead that v 2b be understood as a misplacement created by a scribe confused by the repetition of words and phrases. Mays would read *yigzᵉlû* for *gōzᵉlû* and place it after 3a. This reading of the text is the most plausible approach to

[4] Reading *kiš'ēr* with LXX in light of the indications of synonymous parallelism with compensation and the reference to *šᵉ'ēr* in 2b.

[5] See J. Lindblom, *Micha literarisch untersucht* (Abo: Abo Akademi, 1929) 69–73.

the data and makes sense of the *'āz* at the beginning of verse 4, which otherwise is somewhat puzzling.

The result of this reading is a typical judgment speech that carries its power and force by the careful correspondence of judgment to the sin. The accusation or indictment begins with a general denunciation (1b–2a) and then spells that out via metaphor rather than specific crimes. One is reminded of Amos 5:7, 10–11, which also begins in a general indictment against those who pervert justice.

The description "haters of good and lovers of evil" is reminiscent of Amos's exhortation in Amos 5:15. The elaboration of the sin of the leaders is via a vivid description of the way "they eat the flesh of my people" (cf. Ps 14:4), i.e., the poor. A detailed picture of cannibalism is laid out—strip off the skin, break the bones, chop up the flesh like meat for a cauldron. All this is a way of describing the terrible deeds of injustice wrought by the leaders of Israel against the weak.[6]

The announcement of judgment follows then in vv 2b and 4. In v 2b it is couched in virtually the same language as the indictment, indicating that the cruel treatment the leaders inflict on the weak will be their own fate. They too will be eaten up: their flesh (*šᵉʾēr*—cf. vv 2b, 3, and the LXX of 3b), their bones (*'aṣmōtêhem*, vv 3 and 2b), and "their skin from off them" (*'ôrām mā'ᵃlêhem*, vv 3 and 2b). Their judgment is appropriate in *kind* and *degree* to their sin. The indication that they are to incur the treatment they have rendered the poor is pressed even further in v 4 where one of the primary categories of Old Testament ethics appears—the outcry of the oppressed. When the poor, the weak, the oppressed cry out for help to Yahweh, he will hear and answer because he is compassionate (see Exod 22:22, 26; 3:7—*ṣā'aq*; Ps 22:6—*zā'aq*). But when the oppressors of the poor, those doing evil, cry out in their distress, Yahweh will not answer. A contrast is intended between the final result of the sin—compassion for those in distress as manifest in the judgment against the wicked—and the final result of the judgment—no compassion for those in distress as manifest in Yahweh's failure to answer and turning his face from the wicked.

Micah 3:5–7

(5) Thus says Yahweh concerning the prophets,
the ones leading my people astray,
the ones biting with their teeth
and proclaiming: "Peace!";
but whoever does not put (something) into their mouths,
against him they declare war.
(6) Therefore, it shall be night to you without vision,
and darkness (*ḥᵃšēkāh*) to you without divination.

[6] "The metaphor uncovers the vicious nature of the economic and legal processes by which the powerless are devoured" (Mays, *Micah*, 79).

The sun shall go down on the prophets
and the day shall be dark over them.
(7) The seers shall be ashamed,
and the diviners abashed;
And all of them shall cover their lip,
for there is no answer from God.

These verses comprise yet another judgment speech from Micah, the second in a series of three in this chapter, all of which manifest the correspondence style in one form or another. The previous passage uses a metaphor of cannibalism to work out a detailed correspondence between sin and punishment. This judgment speech has affinities with Amos 7:16 and 17 and Hos 4:4–10 in that it is directed against the religious leaders—prophets in this case—because of the misuse of their office.

The indictment is straight-forward. The prophets lead the people astray by announcing good words to those who support them and feed them and bad words against those who do not do so. In other words, they have used the prophetic office and the prophetic word and vision for their own welfare and material good. In so doing they have misled the people.

The punishment for such a misuse of the office is appropriate to the crime. The means by which they have abused the prophetic role—visions and divination—will be taken from them. And the divine word, which they claim to put forth will not be given to them. They will be disgraced and put to shame. All of this, however, will be part of a larger disaster. The activities of the prophets will bring judgment upon all the people. The night that gives no vision is the darkness of doom that will shatter all (cf. Amos 5:18–20). The prophets' false prophesying brings upon the people a judgment and disaster in which they participate. The reference to covering the lips is to mourning (Lev 13:45; Ezek 24:17, 22) in the time of dark destruction. The absence of an answer from God means not only that the prophets have no word from God any longer, but also that there is no answering word of assurance to the cries in times of trouble.

The passage bears comparison with the judgment against Amaziah, priest of Bethel (Amos 7:16–17). There, too, the crime is the word of the official that misleads, or in this case seeks to thwart the will of God. And his punishment has to do with the ways in which he will be stripped of the office he has misused. He will die on an unclean land and his wife become a harlot—a fate similar to the disgrace of the prophets. Further, his fate is, like that of the prophets against whom Micah announces judgment, a part of a larger suffering of the people which is explicitly announced in Amos 7:17.

Points of comparison may also be noted in relation to Hos 4:4–10, where the priests are castigated for misleading the people and lose their office as judgment upon them. The contrast between day and night appears in verse 5, and verses 7 to 10 characterize the sin of the priests as using their office to feed and support themselves well, as do the prophets whom Micah attacks.

Once again, therefore, the prophets are seen to announce divine judgment upon the leaders appropriate to the nature of their sin. The position they have abused will be the source of judgment upon them. And the judgment they experience will be a part of the judgment rendered upon the whole people.

Micah 3:9–12

(9) Hear this, heads of the house of Jacob,
and rulers of the house of Israel,
the ones who abhor justice
and pervert all the right,
(10) building Zion with blood
and Jerusalem with wrong.
(11) Her heads render decisions for a bribe;
her priests give instruction for a price;
and her prophets divine for money.
Yet they lean on Yahweh, saying,
"Is not Yahweh in our midst?
No disaster will come upon us."
(12) Therefore, because of you
Zion shall be plowed as a field;
Jerusalem shall become a heap of ruins;
and the mount of the house wooded heights.

This example continues Micah's denunciation of the injustice of the leaders of Judah. Once again it is a judgment speech that begins the indictment by describing the accused ones in normative terms and then spelling out in detail what the crimes are (cf. 3:1–4; Amos 5:7, 10–11). The transition between the general and the particular is a bicolon that characterizes the sinners as:

"those who build *Zion* with blood
and *Jerusalem* with wrong" (3:10).

Then in the announcement of punishment is the divine declaration that:

Zion shall be plowed as a field;
Jerusalem shall become a heap of ruins (v 12).

A similar expression to the indictment appears in Hab 2:12:

Woe to him who builds a city with blood,
and founds a town with wrong.

Micah's word of judgment makes clear that a city built in sin will be destroyed in judgment.

In this case we meet an example of what we find elsewhere in Isaiah and Jeremiah. What the people do not think or expect will happen does happen. But the corresponding judgment is not primarily in relation to that expectation as in Isaiah and Jeremiah but in relation to the sin of social injustice, although there is an implicit connection between the assumption: "Is not the Lord in the midst of us?" and the announcement that the grounds for that assumption—Zion—will be destroyed. The event of judgment is apparently military disaster. Northing is said explicitly about the action of Yahweh though it may be assumed. The judgment is not described as happening *out of the sin* but "because of you" and your sin and corresponding to it.

Micah 7:4

> The best of them is like a briar,
> the most upright of them like[7] a hedge;
> The day of their (Heb. equals your) watchmen, their (Heb. equals your) visitation comes;
> Now will be their confusion.

Happily, the textual problems of this verse do not affect the stylistic use of the correspondence device to relate crime and punishment. The verse is part of a larger unit (vv 1–6), possibly post-exilic, which describes the sins of the people in the form of a lament rather than a judgment speech. Verse 4 "in its first half summarizes the denunciation up to the present point, and in its second half threatens the wicked oppressors with punishment."[8] By means of a simile the prophet derides their virtue. The precise point of the comparison can be debated, but it is clearly a negative one consonant with the announcement in v 2 that there is no upright one left. The punishment is then announced in verse 4b as a day of visitation (*p^e^qûdāh*) which will be a time of *m^e^bûkāh*. The correspondence between sin and punishment occurs at this point in the form of a wordplay between one of the words characterizing their sin, i.e., *m^e^sûkāh* and one characterizing their punishment, *m^e^bûkāh*. Both words are unusual and rare and are clearly used here because of the paranomasia they provide. Because of *m^e^sûkāh* there will be *m^e^bûkāh*. One is reminded of a similar form of the correspondence between sin and judgment in Isa 7:9.[9]

So in this passage judgment is again related to sin, but the correspondence is in no sense literal, the deed of punishment being the same as the deed of sin; nor does it involve the instrument of sin. The appropriateness is intentionally contrived to remind the reader of the inherent connection between sin and judgment. In hearing the word of judgment one can relate it immediately back to the sin that brought it forth. But that is not because the seed is planted in the deed. It is only as the wordplay is created that an

[7] M. Dahood, *Psalms III* (Garden City, NY: Doubleday & Company, Inc., 1970) 436.

[8] J. Smith, W. Ward, and J. A. Bewer, *Micah, Zephaniah* . . . (ICC; Edinburgh: T. & T. Clark, 1912) 142.

[9] The other use of *m^e^bûkāh* also involves a wordplay (with *m^e^hûmāh* and *m^e^bûsāh*) in an announcement of judgment (Isa 22:5).

explicit connection is made between the present character of those described and their future punishment, a punishment which is described elliptically, but in light of the vocabulary (e.g., "your watchman," "confusion") and comparison to Isa 22:5ff. must be a military disaster. That which comes in the processes of history as the judgment of God is interpreted or announced as judgment for this sin, this condition. Or vice versa, this sin will bring forth an appropriate judgment, that appropriateness being indicated by play on words rather than literally.

Isaiah

The rhetorical and theological exploitation of the correspondence pattern is nowhere more extensive than in Isa 1–39. Virtually every way of correlating sin and punishment is set forth in these chapters and particularly in what is generally regarded as Isaianic material. The first chapter provides three examples of its own, though one case (1:19–20) is a little different from the other types of correspondence under examination here yet with sufficient similarity to them to warrant inclusion in the discussion.

Isaiah 1:19–20

These verses are set in the form of a legal process of some sort, presumably a hearing to determine the facts of the case, which in the larger context can be seen to function as a judgment speech (so Wildberger). Verses 19–20 offer the possibilities of either blessing or curse[1] and tie these together as well as to the action that determines them by typical Isaianic wordplay:

> (19) If you are willing (*tō'bû*) and obedient,
> you shall eat (*tō'kēlû*) the good (*ṭûb*) of the land.
> (20) But if you refuse and rebel,
> you shall be eaten (*t*^{e}*'ukk*^{e}*lû* by the sword;
> for the mouth of the Lord has spoken.

A correlation of good conduct and good reward is set up in v 19 with the wordplay between *tō'bû* and *ṭûb*. In other words the linguistic device serves to sharpen for the hearers the connection between the fruits of the covenant (*ṭûb*) and obedience to the covenant (*tō'bû*). To paraphrase: If you will be good you will get good.[2] The wordplay connects the conduct or righteousness with the reward and both with the covenantal tradition.[3]

[1] On the covenantal character of the language here, particularly *'ābāh šāma'*, and *ṭôb* see H. Wildberger, *Jesaja* (BKAT; Neukirchen-Vluyn: Neukirchener Verlag, 1972) 53. One could compare also the choice that is placed before the people in such covenantal contexts as Deut 30 and Joshua 24.

[2] A quite similar play on words is found in 7:9 (see below).

[3] In this connection one may compare the Nerab I stele, ll. 11–14 as an example of a similar sort of positive correspondence between good conduct and reward which depends upon repetition of verbs rather than wordplay:

> But if you guard (*nṣr*) this picture and grave,
> in the future may yours be guarded (*nṣr*).

Further correlation is made by the prophet, not between sin and punishment but between reward and punishment. They are made opposite sides of the same coin. If covenant obedience is to eat the good of the land—as indeed it literally is (see Deuteronomy *passim*)—for the prophet disobedience to the covenant (*mārāh, mā'an*) is the reverse of that, i.e. to be eaten. Both consequences involve eating, consuming. In the case of obedient action, however, the people are the subjects of the eating, and it is blessing and reward; while in the case of disobedient action the people are the objects of the eating, and it is curse and punishment.

The concluding clause is not unimportant because it declares that these relationships between deeds and consequences, which are linguistically connected closely together, happen because Yahweh has so decreed. Yahweh as the speaker is the one who makes the linguistic relationships and holds them together.

Isaiah 1:21–26

In this unit a lament in the form of a funeral elegy has been formulated as, or turned into, an indictment of Jerusalem for her crimes. The harlotry image is used briefly but not in the sense of Hosea and Jeremiah to indicate apostasy. The sin of Jerusalem is injustice, the presence of murder, robbery, bribery, and oppression of the weak in the city of David. Two images are used in v 22 to express a single notion about what has happened in the city:

> Your silver has become dross;
> your (choice) liquor/wine weakened with water.

In short, what was pure has become impure. The imagery certainly refers to the *mišpāṭ* and *ṣedeq* of Jerusalem which, once pure and whole, have now become impure and weakened.

When the announcement of judgment is given in vv 24–26, the same imagery is used, but with only one of the examples given in v 22—alloyed precious metal. Judgment and punishment are clearly what is announced here as v 24b indicates with its *hôy*, the reference to Jerusalem and its people as enemies and foes of Yahweh, and the characterization of the action as *nāqam*. They are enemies of Yahweh because they have not kept Yahweh's righteousness and justice right and just. So Yahweh will vindicate himself and maintain his righteousness and justice against them.

But this punishment is correlated with the imagery of the sin, and an important clue to the nature and purpose of divine judgment is thereby given. Verse 25 reads:

Cf. the treaty of Muwattališ and Alakšandus of Wiluša IV 37–44 cited by Lohfink, "Zu Text und Form . . .", 319;

> Wenn du aber diese Worte bewahrst (*paḫḫašti*), so sollen diese tausend Götter . . . dich . . . gütig beschützen (*paḫsantaru*).

> I will turn my hand against you;
> I will smelt away your dross in a smelting-pot;[4]
> I will remove all your alloy.

The sin of Israel is to have let her precious pure silver become alloyed and impure. The punishment is a reversal of that process. Israel will be placed again in the fire not simply as punishment, though that is also going on (cf. Ezek 22:17–22). There is a further ultimate purpose, however, and that is to make Israel pure again, her justice and righteousness unalloyed, unweakened with murder, robbery, bribery, and injustice of every sort. It is Yahweh's intention by this punishment to refine and make her what she was before. That purpose is elaborated in v 26:

> I will restore your judges as at the first[5]
> and your counselors as at the beginning.
> Afterwards you will be called city of righteousness, (*haṣṣedeq*)
> the faithful city (*qiryāh ne'ᵉmānāh*).

Her former state had been that of the faithful city (*qiryāh ne'ᵉmānāh*, v 21) in which righteousness (*ṣedeq*, v 21) lodged, where judges and rulers judged with justice. Yahweh's refining fire will restore her to that pure original state described in v 21.

The correlation, therefore, of sin and judgment, which is effected by an image, does much more than simply point to a surface relationship between the two. Nor is it primarily designed to manifest an ironic poetic justice as, for example, in Amos 6:1–7 and numerous other places. The image of correspondence penetrates into the deepest levels of the nature and purpose of divine judgment. The metaphor of the refining fire that purifies as it punishes is used elsewhere in the prophets (e.g. Isa 48:10 and Ezek 22:17–22; Jer 6:27–30; 9:6–8; Zech 13:9; Mal 3:1–4). It points with clarity to the purposeful nature of judgment and punishment that may be present—though not necessarily. This is the refining fire, not the devouring fire. It is like the dish that is wiped clean, the wall that is torn down and rebuilt to make it straight (1 Kgs 21:13 and elsewhere). The aim of the judgment is to make God's people as they were before: just, righteous, and faithful. The silver cannot be pure again unless the alloys and impurities are removed from it. Such an image also points to the communal character of the experience of judgment. Purification cannot take place here and there, removing the alloy or impurities while leaving the silver alone. The silver as a whole must go through the smelting furnace. Jerusalem in its entirety must experience the *nāqam* of Yahweh to restore her to her pure state. But out of the fires of judgment which all will undergo will come a purified people.

[4] Reading *bakkur* for *kabbōr*, though the text may be correct as it stands, *bōr* meaning "lye", "potash", an alkali used in smelting metals. H. Wildberger, *Jesaja*, 56.

[5] On the possible period Isaiah has in mind with "at the first" (Davidic?) see Wildberger, *Jesaja*, 65–66.

Isaiah 1:29–31

(29) For you shall be put to shame[6] because of
the terebinths (*'êlîm*)
which you have desired;
and you shall be ashamed because of the
gardens (*hagganôt*)
which you have chosen.
(30) For you shall be like a terebinth (*'ēlāh*)
whose leaf withers
and like a garden (*gannāh*) without water.
(31) And the strong one shall be tow,
and his work the spark;
They shall both burn together,
and no one to quench them.

The use of metaphor and simile out of the description of Israel's (Judah's) sin to announce the punishment against her appears again in the final oracle of chapter 1. These verses are altogether an announcement of judgment, but in the first verse of the announcement the sin of the people is indicated. The reason for judgment is the people's delight in setting up Canaanite cultic places and objects of veneration or for cultic use. The *'ēlāh* (terebinth? oak?) is elsewhere condemned as part of pagan shrines. Ezekiel 6:13 speaks of the leafy oak along with the green tree as the place where "they offered pleasing odor to all their idols." Hosea also cites as an example of the harlotry of Israel their sacrifices under oak, poplar, and terebinth (4:13). Deutero-Isaiah mentions both the oak as a place of pagan sexual practices (57:5) and the gardens as places of sacrifice, eating of swine's flesh, and other manifestations of non-Yahwistic worship.

The reference to the desire and choice of *'êlîm* and *gannōt* is quite clear and explicitly indicates worship practices abhorrent to Yahweh and Yahwism. Then the judgment is elaborated in verse 30 by the use of the two similes which directly play on the key words of the description of sin, although in this case *'elāh* is chosen along with *gannāh* rather than *'ayil*. They will become like what in their sin and shame they desire, but the terebinths and gardens of their fate are quite different from those they covet and enjoy. The modifying clauses turn the desirable object of their sin into a simile of their death. The catchwords *'ayil/'elāh* and *gannāh* thus become symbols that identify at one and the same time crime and punishment and correlate the two figuratively but precisely. The two words, as we have seen, are terms for Israel's sin. By this vivid simile Isaiah makes these terms do double duty and point to the judgment they bring about.

It is not altogether certain that verse 31 was originally part of the oracle unit vv 29–30. But in this context if not originally the case, the two have been brought together and interact with each other. Another metaphor altogether is

[6] Reading *tēbōšû* for MT *yēbōšû* (So also Wildberger, Kaiser, BH[3] and others).

created that also correlates sin and punishment. It is not unimportant in the larger discussion because it conveys as vividly perhaps as any image in the prophets the *Tun-Ergehen* relationship, the *schicksalwirkender Tat*. As it correlates sin and punishment in terms of the deed that brings about one's destruction, it draws the correspondence of vv 29–31, at least to some extent, into that same sphere. The strong one in this context has to refer back to those addressed in 29–30 and his work is the desiring of the trees and gardens and the activity that takes place there.[7] That work is the spark that sets off the conflagration. The strong one is consumed by his own work or by the judgment that activity sets off. This metaphor out of the natural world points to a close connection between deed and consequence and an apparent inevitable or natural movement from the former to the latter. No mention is made of divine activity or judgment but one cannot make too much of that. The preceding oracle announces the judgment as Yahweh's wrath and Yahweh's vengeance. The spark to the tow cannot be pressed to speak of a relationship outside of God's decision to turn his hand against them. And, as Wildberger has noted, the expression *'ên mᵉkabbeh* in other contexts (Amos 5:6; Jer 4:4; 21:12) is used where the activity of the divine wrath is described.

Isaiah 3:16–4:1

Isaiah's denunciation of the women of Jerusalem has often been compared to Amos's pronouncement against the fat cows of Bashan (4:1–3). Amos articulates more specifically the involvement of the women in the social sins of Israel. Isaiah paints a stronger picture of the women who, apart from the impetus they give to their husbands' deeds of oppression, are themselves haughty, preening, wanton, and pretentious in their dress and behavior. While the prophet does not in this instance rely upon wordplay, images, or repetition of key terms, he does spell out in detail and quite explicitly the divine punishment appropriate to their sin.[8] The indictment is laid against them because of their manner of bearing and their dress, their physical appearance and what they wear (v 16). Their punishment will be a change in both physical appearance and dress.[9] Those who preened themselves haughtily to look beautiful and attract the glances and attention of men will be made ugly. Instead of haughty good looks, fine clothes, and jewelry, the daughters of Zion will have scabs on their heads and their private parts exposed (assuming that is what *pōt* refers to). The correlation of punishment to sin is specifically indicated in v 24:

[7] In light of the many relationships between Amos and Isaiah it may not be irrelevant that the only other usage of *hāsôn* is in Amos 2:9 where it appears in a simile with *'allôn*, "oak" which is paired elsewhere with *'ēlāh* (Hos 4:13; Isa 6:13).

[8] Cf. Wolff, "Die Begründungen . . ." 21ff.

[9] Verses 18–23 may be a later insertion. They do not, however, violate the correspondence between sin and punishment that is intended in the unit.

Instead of perfume there will be rottenness;
instead of girdle, rope.
Instead of well-set hair, baldness;
and instead of rich robe, a girding of sack-cloth
Yea, instead of beauty . . .[10]

The manifestation of their sin will become the locus of judgment.[11] The following verses describe a scene of destruction and death. Verses 17 and 24 (and 4:1) show how the women will participate in that judgment as their condition is dramatically reversed. Sickness, death, and mourning will turn the proud and beautiful to shame and ugliness. Fine dress will be changed to the mean dress of mourning.

All this is Yahweh's doing (v 17). In the judgment that he will bring upon the people the haughty women will experience a punishment closely correlated to their sin.

Isaiah 5:8–10

(8) Woe, the ones joining house to house,
who connect field to field,
until there is no more room and you are made to dwell
alone in the midst of the land.
(9) In my ears Yahweh of hosts . . .
Surely many houses great and beautiful
shall be desolate without inhabitant,
(10) For ten acres of vineyard shall yield one balk
and a homer of seed shall yield an ephah.

Even though Isaiah frequently uses wordplay, metaphor, simile, and repetition of verbs, as the previous text indicates, the prophetic announcement of judgment may correspond to the sin of the accused quite substantively. A further example is found here in a passage that has affinities with two previous passages discussed: Amos 5:7, 10–11 and Mic 2:1–5. In these verses we encounter a correlation of sin and judgment through what Hillers has called the futility curse, coming out of treaty and covenant style and traditions.

The accusation couched in the form of a woe oracle is an indictment of those in Judah who were practicing a form of early capitalism[12] involving the rapid expansion of one's wealth by acquiring more and more houses and land. The result was a breakdown in the order of Israelite society, increasing

[10] The translation of this colon is uncertain. IQIs^{a} adds "shame."

[11] Cf. Wolff, "Die Begründungen . . ."

[12] In a paper read to a 1976 regional meeting of the SBL entitled "Social Justice: Perspectives from the Prophetic Tradition," James L. Mays characterizes this early capitalism as: "the shift of the primary social good, land, from the function of support to that of capital; the reorientation of social goals from personal values to economic profit; the subordination of judicial process to the interests of the entrepreneur."

discrepancy between rich and poor, and a fundamental violation of Yahweh's intention for the relationship between people and land. The houses and land brought increased affluence and luxury as well as increasing amounts of produce from the land. How the houses and land were acquired we are not told. Presumably "legal" means were often used, but the law as Yahweh's instruction for Israel's life was violated in its intention. The land as Yahweh's gift with each family having its inheritance or allotted portion as a basis for existence became less and less the norm.[13]

The correlation of sin and judgment involves repetition of words but not altogether. Nor is the repetition a matter of the judgment being a reversal of the sin. The correspondence is one of result or frustration of result. The two foci of the accusation correspond to the two foci of the announcement of punishment: houses and fields. Those who join house to house (v 8a) will experience an appropriate judgment. The sin of greedy acquisition of many fine houses means the judgment of not being able to live in them (v 9a), i.e. exile or death. In like manner a similar fate awaits those who against Yahweh's will "add a field to field" (8a). The intention of such land acquisition is to enlarge one's productive property and thereby one's wealth. But the judgment on those who commit this sin is that the object of their sinful greed will leave them poverty stricken. The fields acquired will yield little (v 10).

The resultant picture of the fate of the land-grabbers is one of exile and poverty. The basis of the punishment is the covenant and the invoking of the covenant curses (cf. Lev 26:20 and 32 and Deut 28:30 and 28).[14] It is not accidental that the covenant curses are spelled out here in a modified form. Their correspondence or appropriateness for the sin surely lies behind their being invoked in this judgment speech.[15] Or alternatively one may say that the presence of such curses in the covenantal tradition evokes or helps to formulate the indictment given here.

[13] "The central problem was the ownership of land and the benefits and rights that went with it in Israelite society. Land was being accumulated in estates and used as a basis for status and to generate surplus wealth. Those who lost their land were deprived of status and material support. They had to become slaves or wage laborers to live. The leverage employed was the administrative apparatus of the monarchy and the courts. The rights of the widow, fatherless, and weak to protection against the economic process were widely ignored. The result was a growing differentiation between rich and poor." Mays, "Social Justice: Perspectives from the Prophetic Tradition."

[14] On the covenantal character of *l^e^šammāh yihyû* and the verb *šāmam* with reference to Deut 28:37 and Lev 26:22, 31f. see Wildberger, *Jesaja*, 185.

[15] Cf. the comment of Wildberger: "die Strafe sich im selben Bereich auswirkt, in dem der Frevel begangen wurde . . ." (*Jesaja*, 185). Wolff notes the correspondence here but discusses it entirely in terms of the repetition of *bayit* without reference to the further correspondence regarding the fields. Even though the word *śādeh* is not repeated, the correspondence is substantially of the same sort as that pertaining to the houses.

Isaiah 7:9

The phenomenon of wordplay as a way of correlating sin and judgment has its classic manifestation in Isa 7:9, Isaiah's words to Ahaz in the face of the Syro-Ephraimite threat. The passage is so familiar it needs no elaboration but should at least be cited. The prophetic word is a conditional one, announcing the fateful consequence if Ahaz does not do what he should:

> *'im lō' ta'ᵃmînu ki lō' tē'āmēnû.*

The potential sin is *lō' ta'ᵃmînû*; the inevitable consequence or punishment for that sin will be *lō' tē'āmēnû.* "If you will not stand firm, you will not be stood firm." The familiarity and cleverness of the wordplay should not be allowed to obscure what the prophet accomplishes by his rhetoric. The issue is wrapped up in all that *'āmēn* means. In a sense the prophet says if you do not do this, it will not be done to you. If Ahaz does not act in the knowledge that Yahweh and his promises are firm, then he and his future will not be firm. God will not secure the one who does not regard him as secure. The historical context gives to this correspondence the sense of the fate-creating deed. For Ahaz's failure to trust in the prophetic word and the divine promises sows the seeds of fateful and unhappy fruit for Judah.

Isaiah 8:5–8

The correlation of sin and punishment in 8:5–8 depends upon the key word *mayim* and the changes it undergoes through the modifying words and phrases. A metaphor is used to describe the people's sin and then modified or transformed to announce the judgment. It has affinities in various respects, therefore, with 1:19–20, 29–31, and 5:8–10 but is not quite the same thing as any one of them.

The accusation in the judgment speech is a strange one and has one major textual problem in v 6b. The clause *ûmᵉ'sôs 'et-rᵉṣôn ûben rᵉmalyāhû* makes no sense in the context if "this people" in v 6a refers to Judah, as it surely does. Hardly any scholar accepts the MT as it stands, but all the proposals for emendation are quite problematic.[16] Lindblom and Kaiser interpret 6b differently but both see it as the judgment for the sin in 6a. That goes against the context which clearly demands that Pekah and Rezin in some fashion have to do with Judah's sin and Assyria with the judgment against her (see chapter 7). Furthermore, the *lākēn* of v 7 clearly signals the beginning of the announcement of judgment in which Yahweh is designated as the one bringing about the judgment.

In the absence of a means of improving 6b, it should be left untranslated. Unless one reads it as the announcement of judgment, the

[16] See the discussions in ICC, Wildberger, *Jesaja*, and J. Lindblom, *A Study on the Immanuel Section in Isaiah*, 43ff.

point under discussion does not depend on it. Further, the observation being made in the context of the other examples in Isaiah and elsewhere confirms the fact that the announcement of judgment begins at v 7.

The sin of the people is a refusal of the gently flowing "waters of Shiloah" (*mê haššilōaḥ*). It is generally recognized that the expression, "the waters of Shiloah," refers to an open channel that "conducted the water from the Gihon spring along the western Kidron-slope for irrigation of its cultivated terraces and for supplying the inhabitants of the city with water."[17] The expression is not used elsewhere and must be a metaphor in this case. Its precise reference or meaning is hard to determine. It would appear to refer to a rejection by the people of the calm, caring, life-sustaining help of Yahweh that is available to them where they are.[18]

In any event because the sin is to refuse[19] the gentle waters in their midst that sustain them, the punishment is to receive the flooding waters from afar that ultimately overwhelm them and destroy them. No, to the *mê haššilōaḥ* means that Yahweh will bring upon them the waters of Euphrates, *mê hannāhār*, which are *hā ʿaṣûmîm weha-rabbîm* in contrast to the *mê haššilōaḥ* which are *le'aṭ*. Both accusation and announcement of punishment use symbolic language and the symbols correspond but are contrasted by their respective modifiers producing a metaphorical correspondence between the sin and the punishment.

The agent of the punishment is Yahweh, and while the expression of it is metaphorical, the metaphor is perfectly consistent in its meaning with the prophetic view of history as the context in which Yahweh works out his redemptive and judging purposes through the movement of history. Indeed, the announcement of judgment found its reality in subsequent history as the *mê hannāhār* flowed on into Judah and overwhelmed it (cf. 7:18–20).

One can see on the historical plane how the sin brings about the punishment, but the passage, which makes a stylistic connection with the image of the waters, creating a sense of the appropriate judgment, breaks any easy notion of the consequence immanent in the deed by the forthright statement that Yahweh will bring about the judgment.[20]

Isaiah 28:1–4

Chapters 28–33 of Isaiah make up a section within the book that is ordered primarily around a series of woe-sayings at the beginning of the chapters.[21] Most of these woe-sayings are characterized by the phenomenon

[17] Lindblom, *A Study . . .*, 43.

[18] Wildberger, *Jesaja*, 325 would see here a rejection of the divine word.

[19] On the use of *mā'as* in cases of correspondence and its possible covenantal connotations see Lohfink, "Zu Text und Form . . .", 320ff.

[20] Cf. Herbert Donner, *Israel unter den Völker* (Leiden: E. J. Brill, 1964), 25.

[21] Chapter 32 does not begin with a woe-saying, while 29:15 begins another woe-saying within that chapter.

of correspondence of some sort between the description of the sin and the description of the punishment[22] and such a correlation may also be found elsewhere in this section of Isaiah. The correspondence may be very precise and literal (e.g. 33:1ff.) or it may involve an allusion in the *hôy* sentence which does not necessarily refer to the sin but which is picked up in the announcement of punishment (e.g. 29:1ff.).

The first case of correspondence in the section is the initial unit, 28:1–4. The exact historical setting is debated,[23] but it appears to be an oracle directed against Israel and Samaria prior to the fall of that city. The *hôy* is against "the proud crown (*'ᵃṭeret*) of the drunkards of Ephraim and the fading flower of its glorious beauty (*ṣᵉbî tip'artô*) which is on the head of the rich valley of those stricken with wine." The reference is to Samaria, and the denunciation is reminiscent of Amos 6:1ff. which describes at greater length, while making the same point, "the proud and besotted nobles of Samaria."[24] The capitol city with its arrogant and drunken princes will be destroyed by Yahweh's agent "mighty and strong" (v 2). The allusion is undoubtedly to an Assyrian ruler who will come with devastating force like a mighty storm against Ephraim and Samaria. As the announcement of judgment continues in verses 3 and 4, it picks up quite explicitly the imagery of the woe-saying which served as an indictment:

> The proud crown of the drunkards of Ephraim
> shall be trodden underfoot;
> And the fading flower of its glorious beauty
> which is on the head of the rich valley shall be
> as a first-ripe fig before the summer;
> whoever sees it,
> as soon as it is in his hand, he shall eat it.

The correspondence here is purely figurative. The double image created in the woe-saying becomes the vehicle for the word of judgment. The proud crown will be torn off by Yahweh's mighty one and smashed under foot. The second metaphor of the fading flower is extended into a simile of the first ripe fig that is immediately gobbled up. The very extension of the image, so that while one is still confronted with the realm of flora the

[22] W. Janzen, *Mourning Cry and Woe Oracle*, 35ff. has pointed out this characteristic in the OT woe oracles. More recently G. Nickelsburg, "The Apocalyptic Message of *I Enoch* 92–105," *CBQ* 39 (1977) 310ff. has noted the phenomenon also in some woe-sayings in The Book of Enoch.

[23] See the discussion in O. Kaiser, *Isaiah 13–39*, (Philadelphia: Westminster, 1974) 237ff. But his very late setting is too forced and involves a literalizing of the imagery that in this case is unlikely and unnecessary. See now the discussion of Wildberger, *Jesaja*, 1045–46, who regards the unit as Isaianic and from the period between the Syro-Ephraimite war of 733 and Shalmaneser's siege of Samaria in 725/24.

[24] J. Bright, "Isaiah-I", *Peake's Commentary on the Bible* (London: Thomas Nelson & Sons, 1962), 508.

images have become mixed, indicates in this example that the prophet is interested more in the correlation of sin and punishment as a rhetorical and prosodic device than a sharp theological statement of talionic character, which indeed it is not. Confirmation of the force of the correspondence and the way it is functioning is found in the immediately following verse 5. This may well be an insertion, a later addition, not by the prophet who announced the judgment of vv 1–4. But whether by the original speaker or the work of a later hand, verse 5 picks up the catch words of the woe-saying and the announcement of judgment (*ʿᵃṭeret, ṣᵉbî, tipʾārāh*) and uses them in a salvation word about the future:

> In that day Yahweh *Ṣᵉbaʾot* will be
> a crown of beauty,
> A diadem glory for the remnant of his people.

The proud crown of Ephraim is punished for its sin and trodden under foot. Beyond the judgment, however, the remnant of Yahweh's people will be given a new crown, the Lord of Hosts, to replace the sinful crown.

Thus imagery shared by words of indictment, judgment, and salvation serve to create a correlation among them and a unity of all three.

Isaiah 28:7–13

Walther Zimmerli cites another example of Isaiah's turning the sin back upon the sinner as judgment in Isa 28:7–13. In vv 7–8 Isaiah attacks priest and prophet as too drunk to give *torah* and the vision of the Lord to the people. In response to Isaiah's rebuke, however, they mock him:

> (9) Whom shall he teach knowledge,
> and to whom shall he explain the message?
> Those weaned from the milk,
> those taken from the breast?
> (10) For it is *ṣaw* for *ṣaw*, *ṣaw* for *ṣaw*,
> *qaw* for *qaw*, *qaw* for *qaw*,
> a little here, a little there. (vv 9–10)

In other words they derisively ask who is he to teach us. His words are like a schoolteacher, teaching the ABCs to children or monotonously repeating a lesson.

Whereupon the prophet announces to them:

> (11) With stammerings of lip and with another tongue
> he shall speak to this people,
> (12) to whom he has said,
> "This is rest;
> give rest to the weary;
> and this is repose."
> But they were unwilling to listen.

In other words Yahweh will address this people who have not listened to his good news about finding their trust and true resting place in him with words which for them are an unknown tongue, which are for them *saw* for *saw*, *qaw* for *qaw*.[25] Or as John Bright puts it with blunt eloquence: "Very well, since you will not hear Yahweh's lesson spelled out in plain Hebrew, it will be taught you in Assyrian."[26] Yahweh has taught you often enough to put your trust in him, find your rest in him. You have not learned the lesson and have mocked the prophet as nothing more than a schoolteacher repeating the alphabet over and over to babes. So now Yahweh will indeed teach you your ABCs, only with an Assyrian schoolmaster. And this time, to your dismay, you will get the lesson.

What has been the prophet's description of the leaders, their mocking description of a teacher teaching the basics, becomes a powerfully ironic vehicle for the word of judgment. The prophet accepts the mocking description and announces that the judgment for those who react to the word of God this way—as unimportant children's matters—will be to learn the basics the hard way, under a cruel and tyrannical teacher who will teach them in a powerful language. The correspondence creates a high sense of irony. The catchwords mean the same thing in both accusation and announcement of judgment. What turns them from accusation to announcement is the shift in the person who speaks or teaches the elementals of Yahweh's word.

The message is the same as the word about the "waters of Shiloah"—destruction at the hands of the Assyrians because of failure to trust in Yahweh. The stylistic device of correspondence is worked out in a somewhat similar fashion. But the passage has its own individuality and power as an expression of the prophetic word of judgment with an artfulness and irony that are virtually unsurpassed in prophetic literature.

A final note: The frequency of the correspondence pattern and awareness of its usage has significance for one's literary critical conclusions. Both Donner[27] and Kaiser[28] do not include v 13 as a part of the original unit. They regard it as an artificial construction comprised from v 10 and 8:15. Such a conclusion ignores the widespread character of the correspondence device in Isaianic material, especially chapters 28–33. While it is possible that the verse is later, its relation to v 10 is no reason to suspect that. On the contrary the similarity suggests that it belongs to the oracle, particularly inasmuch as v 13 is the clear word of judgment in the passage.

Isaiah 28:14–18

The third unit of this chapter is a complex one that was probably not originally a unity. Kaiser's analysis best explains the growth of the unit:

[25] Cf. W. Zimmerli, "Verkündigung und Sprache der Botschaft Jesajas," 75–76.

[26] Bright, "Isaiah I," 508. See Wildberger, *Jesaja*, 1053–54 for various interpretations of the enigmatic v 13.

[27] Donner, *Israel unter den Völker*, 148.

[28] Kaiser, *Isaiah*, 244.

> Perhaps the most likely explanation of the growth of the passage is to see it as taking place in three main stages. The first stage was the prophecy by Isaiah to be found in vv 14–15 and 16aα, 17b–18. To this the redactor who can be seen at work particularly in 30:8–17, and perhaps lived before the exile, added vv 16aβb and 17a. Finally, the passage was reinterpreted in an eschatological sense by the addition of vv 20–22. It is no longer possible to tell whether v 19 was inserted at the same time or separately.[29]

If this analysis, which is plausible (but see below), is essentially correct, the basic original unit is vv 14–15, 16a, 17b–18. It is in just those verses, which make up a judgment speech against the rulers of Jerusalem, that one finds a clear correspondence between sin and punishment.

(14) Therefore, hear the word of Yahweh, you scoffers,
rulers of this people who are in Jerusalem.
(15) For you have said: "We have made
a covenant with death,
and with Sheol
we have made a pact.[30]
When the overwhelming flood[31] passes by,
it shall not come upon us;
For we have made *lies* our *refuge*,
and among falsehoods we have *hidden ourselves*,
(16a) Therefore thus says the Lord Yahweh,
(17b) Hail shall sweep away the *refuge* of *lies*;
and water shall *overwhelm the hiding place*.
(18) Then your covenant with death shall be broken;[32]
and your pact with Sheol shall not stand,
The overwhelming flood shall surely[33] pass by;
but you shall be a trampling place for it.

The denunciation of the prophet is here directed against the nobles and aristocracy who scoff at Yahweh's threats against them and think to have made themselves secure, so that they are not in danger of death and destruction as Yahweh's prophet has claimed. The particular reference for

[29] *Ibid.*, 250. See note a for references to further discussion of the literary problems of the unit (cf. the discussion in Wildberger, *Isaiah*). Most scholars see the main part of this unit as coming from the period 713 to 701 probably in the latter part.

[30] The meaning here of *ḥōzeh* and of *ḥāzût* in v 18 is quite uncertain. See the discussion of G. R. Driver, "'Another Little Drink'—Isaiah 28:1–22," *Words and Meanings*, ed. P. R. Ackroyd and B. Lindars (Cambridge: Cambridge University Press, 1968) 58; and Wildberger, *Jeseja*, 1064–65.

[31] On *šwt/šyt* see the discussions of Driver and Wildberger.

[32] Reading *w^{e}tupar* instead of *w^{e}kuppar*. While it is true that *w^{e}kuppar* is *lectio dificilior*, the parallel expression in 8:10, where *w^{e}tupar* appears in parallel with *lō nāqûm* as here and the syntax is comparable, points strongly toward the emended reading. In addition the other uses of the Hophal form *tupar* (Jer 33:21 and Zech 11:11) also have to do with breaking covenant.

[33] The *kî* here is emphatic, casting the verb to the end of the colon. The same may be true of *kî* in v 15b.

the "covenant of death" is unclear. It may refer, as some have suggested, to the Egyptian deities in whose name a pact has been made (so, e.g., J. Bright, who sees the *kāzāb* and *šeqer* as prophetic terms for false gods). The expression may have in mind private agreements made with the Assyrians. Or we may have here simply figurative and metaphorical language whereby the scoffers claim, or act as if they claim, to have warded off Death and Sheol, here almost personified beings. Their sin is to mock the power and control of Yahweh, once again to place their trust elsewhere, and by lies and falsehood (false gods? pacts? assurances to the people?) protect themselves against the flood that will come. They have rejected Yahweh's word through his prophet and scoffed at it (*'anšê lāṣôn*, v 14 and cf. vv 7–13). They do not worry about the flood (Assyrian; cf. 8:5–8) that is to come. At the same time they have taken their refuge elsewhere than in Yahweh. Their sin is a double rejection of the God of Israel.

The judgment that is announced in 16ff. picks up the imagery of the flood of the Assyrian army and takes every element of self-assurance in the indictment of verse 15 and negates it. The overwhelming flood which these scoffers thought would not touch them will come upon them with such force it will make them a trampling-place. (The term *mirmas* conveys the double impact of the image of the flood waters and the reality of the Assyrian army.) The shelter sought in lies will be swept away by this flood. The hiding place away from the overwhelming (*šôṭēp*) flood will itself be overwhelmed (*yištōpû*). The covenant with Death, the pact with Sheol will be demolished. Those whose sin is to seek life apart from Yahweh will find instead death from Yahweh.

So in detailed fashion the prophet uses again, as he did in 8:5–8 images of a conquering army as a powerful flood to express the fact that Yahweh will bring upon his people a judgment appropriate to their sin. It is not that the judgment matches the punishment in some quantitative sense but rather that precisely at the point of their sin they will find the judgment of God. In its simplest terms the sin could be described as ignoring God's warnings and securing protection from the pending danger from some other source; the judgment is that the pending danger will get them anyway. But such a formulation as that misses altogether the inner relation the prophet sees between sin and judgment. It is not quantitative or talionic. Nor does the prophet seem concerned to express a notion that the consequences are sown or inherent in the deed. Rather the prophetic rhetoric serves to heighten the emphasis upon the sin and its character. When he turns from the words of reproach and indictment to the announcement of judgment, he does not set aside now the question of the sin. Nor is the hearer or reader allowed to forget what is at stake or at issue in the divine response. The prophetic judgment speech is designed always to keep before hearers and readers at the time or later the relationship between the earlier sinful deed(s) and the subsequent or later punishment lest they fail to see the connection or forget it. The device of correspondence accomplishes this intention forcefully and inescapably. The divine judgment does not come in a general way or without basis. As the prophet point by point correlates the judgment with the sin, he serves not only to convey an element of irony in the divine governance of the processes of history, but he underscores the human deeds or attitudes that have brought the response and that the response is (appropriate) for these deeds or attitudes.

The judgment itself is wrought out through the agency of the Assyrian army. No special punishment or "act of God" in the language of insurance policies is implied. The Assyrian menace is there and recognized. Indeed the sin of the rulers is to claim to be able to escape it. The judgment announced by the prophet is that they will not escape it. The rod of Yahweh's anger through actions chronicled in Hebrew writings and Assyrian annals will accomplish the divine judgment.[34]

Before leaving this text one should note that the assumption that vv 16aβb and 17a are a later interpolation is not shared by all. Most recently Wildberger[35] and Melugin[36] have questioned the assumption. The latter scholar, who has also perceived the irony in 28:7–13, has suggested that a wordplay centering upon the dual use of the verb *śîm* connects vv 15 and 17a and thus demonstrates the basic unity of vv 14–19. The indictment quotes the scoffers as saying *śamnû kāzāb maḥsēnû*, "We have put lies as our refuge," to which Yahweh in judgment announces *w^eśamtî mišpāṭ l^eqāw*, "I will put justice as the line."[37] Whether or not the verses in dispute are original, Melugin has helped to show that in the present form of the text the correlation of sin and punishment is pervasive and may, as in vv 7–13, suggest that previous literary critical conclusions about earlier and later material will have to be revised.

[34] The following comment by Thorkild Jacobsen shows how the "Lament for Ur" provides an analogy that could be duplicated in numerous other texts:

> Stating in plain terms what we know happened we could say that wild mountaineers from the East—Elam and the Sua people—invaded Sumer, besieged Ur, and when eventually the inhabitants surrendered the city, sacked and burned it mercilessly. But plain terms would be entirely inadequate to convey what the Sumerians knew took place. In a cosmic sense it was Enlil's own destructive essence expressed in his element the storm that destroyed Ur. The wild hordes from the mountains were but incidental form in which that essence clothed itself, the reality was Enlil's storm . . . (*The Treasures of Darkness* [New Haven: Yale University Press, 1976], 88).

[35] Wildberger, *Jesaja*, 1069–1071.

[36] R. F. Melugin, "The Conventional and the Creative in Israel's Judgment Oracles," *CBQ* 36 (1974) 301–11.

[37] *Ibid.*, 309.

Isaiah 29:1–3

These verses are part of the unit 29:1–8 which moves from threat of judgment against Jerusalem to announcement of deliverance. The first three verses encompass the word of judgment. Verse 4 may be a part of this woe saying, but that is less clearly the case.

(1) Woe, Ariel, Ariel,
city where David encamped!
Add year to year;
let the feasts run their round.
(2) I will distress Ariel;
and there shall be mourning and lamentation;
and she shall be to me as Ariel.
(3) I will encamp against you like David;[38]
and I will besiege you with outposts;
and I will raise siegeworks against you. . . .

The correspondence device is worked out in quite different fashion in this instance, reflecting the diversity one finds in Isa 1–39 in the manner in which correlation between sin and punishment is articulated. Verse 1 as a woe-saying would normally function as an indictment or reproach for sin, which then would form the basis for the announcement of punishment. But, as Kaiser has remarked: "Verse 1b fulfills this function in a very unsatisfactory fashion; for why should the people of Jerusalem not celebrate the New Year festival?"[39] The verse identifies the objects of reproach, those who have sinned, as is customary in the opening line of a woe-saying. But it does not identify them in terms of their particular sin as one would normally expect. Rather the woe is uttered and the object identified by a historical reference: "the city where David encamped." Even this allusion is unclear. It may have in mind David's attack on the city or simply point to the fact that it was David's city. The second part of the verse either establishes the time when the judgment will come or indicates that eventually it will come. None of this, however, establishes a proper indictment for sin.

There follows, nevertheless, an announcement of punishment in which correlation of the woe-sentence and the announcement appears. In this case there cannot be demonstrated a punishment that is appropriate to the sin

[38] MT has *kaddûr*, which, as Duhm pointed out, makes little sense as a comparison in this case. Further the very existence of the word *dûr*, "ball, circle," is most uncertain, all the other examples being debatable. It is often said that LXX reading *kdwd* for *kdwr* is simply under the influence of verse 1 and not original. The frequency with which Isaiah makes just such a correspondence and the fact that the correspondence is already present in the use of *ḥānāh* raises questions about that assumption. Further, the palaeographic similarity of *dalet* and *reš* in the seventh-sixth centuries is well known, as witness the debate over reading *gādēr*, "wall, enclosure" or *g*ᵉ*dûd*, "band, troop" on the Gibeon jar handle inscriptions, even though the word appears numerous times.

[39] Kaiser, *Isaiah*, 266.

because the latter has not really been stated. But that which takes its place, the reference to David's encampment, becomes again the trigger that sets off a powerful image of judgment. The latter corresponds, therefore, not to the sin as it is stated, but to that which substitutes for it. In other words a historical reference becomes the basis for the correspondence, rather than an indictment, but it can function that way because it is a part of the element in which normally one finds the sins elaborated in a woe-saying judgment speech (cf. Isa 28:1–6; 33:1; Amos 6:1–7). In other judgment speeches items in the woe-sentence that identify the recipients of judgment are picked up in the judgment word, but regularly they also point to the character of the sin. In this case that which is only an identifying element evokes a particular word of judgment. Where David encamped, Yahweh will encamp. But the preposition *ʿal* in verse 3 eliminates the ambiguity that is in the syntax of the corresponding part in verse 1. This is clearly an encampment *against*, a siege that is laid against Jerusalem. If LXX is correct in verse 3 then the correspondence is carried further and the reference in verse 1 is less ambiguous. As Jerusalem (Ariel) was besieged once before by David, Yahweh will besiege her again.

The one who recapitulates David's earlier actions as a judgment against Israel is clearly and only Yahweh as the singular first person subject of the various verbs indicates (*wah^{a}ṣîqôtî, w^{e}ḥanîtî, w^{e}ṣartî, wah^{a}qîmōtî*). The *divine* initiative and action are what the prophet announces. It is Yahweh's judgment. But as the overwhelming flood which makes Jerusalem and its leaders a trampling place suggests the rush of the mighty Assyrian army, even more so does the announcement of Yahweh's siege against Jerusalem point to the means by which Yahweh will accomplish his judgment in the processes of history—the siege of an Assyrian army. The moment of judgment does not transcend the historical continuum, nor come from outside it. It is not even a surprise. Indeed, familiarity with Assyrian siege practices may be what elicits and shapes the whole of this prophetic word. If the oracle stands in any relation to the events of 701, then the force and reference of the imagery of Yahweh's siege is all too clear. Yet the divine word is that Sennacherib's siege (if that is the one in mind) is to be seen and known as Yahweh's judgment. And the city which Yahweh's king, David, conquered and made the royal and divine dwelling-place will find itself again under siege, this time by the one who chose David.

Isaiah 30:1–5

(1) Woe, the rebellious children,
oracle of Yahweh,
who make a plan, but not mine,
who pour out libations, but not by my spirit,
so as to add sin upon sin;

(2) those who set out to go down to Egypt,
without asking for my counsel
to take refuge in the protection of Pharaoh
and to seek shelter in the shadow of Egypt.
(3) So shall the protection of Pharaoh be for you shame,
and the shelter in the shadow of Egypt humiliation.
(4) For though his princes are at Zoan,
and his messengers reach Hanes,
(5) All have become odious
through a people that does not profit them,
neither help nor profit,
but shame, indeed reproach.

It is possible that verses 6 and 7 are a part of this unit (so Bright) in light of the similarily between the end of v 6 and the beginning of v 7 and the concerns and language of verses 1–5. But there are problems in moving to include these two verses, not least of which is the heading at the beginning of verse 6. It may be that verses 6 and 7 were placed here because of their obvious associations with the content of vv 1–5.

Whether or not that is the case, vv 1–5 demonstrate another Isaianic example of the correlation between sin and judgment. As in the preceding passages the historical context appears to be 705 to 701 B.C., more particularly the effort of the Judeans to secure Egyptian help in revolt against the Assyrians. The sin denounced by Yahweh through his prophet is explicitly rebellion; the children have disobeyed the father. The prophetic word to forego such military alliances has been ignored in disobedience of the divine will. Further, they have sinned by making plans and leagues (assuming that is what is meant by pouring out libations) without consulting Yahweh. They reject his word and turn to other powers for protection in time of trouble. The sin is, therefore, an offense against Yahweh, the primal sin of rebellion against God manifest in turning aside his divine word and trusting in someone else, seeking refuge elsewhere than in the God who is "our refuge and strength" (Ps 46:1), "your shadow on your right hand" (Ps 121:5). Within the Psalter the confession that Yahweh is the refuge of his people, the shadow that shelters them is a common theme (Pss 17:8; 27:1; 28:8; 31:3; 37:39; 38:8; 43:2; 52:9; 57:2; 63:8; 90:1; 91:1; 121:5). Yahweh announces that Judah by her actions has set aside that confession and that relationship. She seeks from human beings what she knows comes from God.[40]

As in Isa 28:14–18 the intention (infinitive construct) of the sin to find security will be thwarted by the judgment of God. Therein lies the correspondence between sin and punishment, that what the people hoped to accomplish by their sin will not happen and what they hoped to avoid will come to pass. The "protection of Pharaoh," (*mā'ôz par'ōh*, v 3); the "refuge

[40] *Ibid.*, 286.

in the shadow of Egypt," (*hāḥāsût b^eṣēl miṣrayim*, v 2) will turn to humiliation. Once again the coming events will be the vehicle of Yahweh's judgment. Egypt is a weak reed and will provide no protection at all. As past events should have indicated,[41] reliance on Egypt will bring greater ignominy on Jerusalem as Assyria smashes that weak reed and vents its wrath against the kingdom that sought Egyptian help. Judah in alliance with Egypt will be humiliated rather than protected, a fate she indeed experienced at the hands of Sennacherib.

The correlation of sin and punishment sharpens the prophetic affirmation that Israel's only refuge is Yahweh. The repetition of *mā'ôz* and *ḥāsût* places those words at the center of attention. The issue at stake in this interaction of sin and judgment is wherein Israel will trust for her security. By relating the punishment to the sin at just that point the issue is laid out with startling clarity.

In this context one should take note that Donner[42] and Kaiser[43] have argued that because verse 3 overlaps with verse 2 and in part with verse 5 it is a later explanatory gloss that does not belong to the original unit. In the margin of the book by Kaiser in the Union Theological Seminary (Richmond) library someone has penciled in lightly by Kaiser's comment to this effect: "Good grief! Why?" While such a reaction may be a bit overdone, one is compelled to challenge the conclusion of Donner and Kaiser, not because such glosses do not appear in the midst of prophetic oracles. Indeed they do. But what is called explanatory gloss in this case is the element of correspondence in the judgment part of the woe-saying, a rhetorical and theological device that we have seen to be common in eighth century prophecy, frequent in Isa 1–39, and indeed almost the rule in Isa 28–33 where at least seven separate oracles manifest this characteristic. Attention to such correspondence in these oracles places the burden of proof on the one who would excise a verse because it shows such correspondence.

Isaiah 30:15–17

(15) For thus said Adonai Yahweh, the Holy One of Israel:
"In returning and rest you shall be saved,
in quietness and in trust shall be your strength;"
But you were unwilling (16) And you said, "No!
We will speed away (*nānûs*) on horses.". . .
Therefore you shall flee (*t^enûsûn*).
And "We will ride on swift (*qal*) steeds."
Therefore your pursuers shall be swift (*yiqqallû*).
(17) A thousand at the threat of one (shall flee)
at the threat of five you shall flee (*tānusû*)

[41] *Ibid.*, 284.
[42] Donner, *Israel unter den Völker*, 132.
[43] Kaiser, *Isaiah*, 282–83.

until you are left
like a flagstaff on the top of a mountain,
like a signal (*nēs*) on a hill.

The judgment speech in this instance depends totally on the way the prophet develops an intricate correlation of sin and punishment. As previous examples have shown, Isaiah rarely uses the simple repetition of verbs indicating punishment as a reversal of the sin. His stylistic application of this pattern is frequently more complex and mixes repetition of words (but not necessarily reversal), wordplay, and figures of speech. Chapter 30:15–17 illustrates this well.

The principal point of correlation is the verb *nûs*, but the correlation depends upon a double meaning to the verb as well as a play on words with another word. In addition a second correlation is created with the verb *qālal* and its adjective *qal*. The sin of the people is their unwillingness[44] to sit quietly and trust in Yahweh to deliver them. Instead they quickly seek after strong military alliances and put their trust in them. Over against the divine demand and assurance, the sin of the people is described in three cola: you were unwilling; you said: "No."; you said: *'al sûs nānûs*. The verb *nûs* is somewhat ambiguous in this instance. Its regular meaing is clearly "flee (from), escape" as from enemies. It could mean here flight to Egypt or elsewhere for help. Or it may simply mean flight as opposed to rest, which is Yahweh's instruction (v 15). The immediate context as well as the larger context suggests more the idea of flying to the attack (so BDB) rather than from it. But it must be said that this is a most unusual meaning for *nûs*.[45]

In any event, with this quotation ascribed to the people the announcement of judgment (*'al kēn*) begins and declares in high irony that the people will get what they want. Those who would flee (whether to the attack or from the enemy) will indeed flee, i.e. impending disaster is at hand. In effect Yahweh says: If you choose to fly rather than to obey and trust, then you will get what you want. But that flight will be judgment rather than salvation. In effect the people's sin will turn into judgment.

A parallel statement of that irony is given in the next line. Judah's sin is to ride on swift horses. Her judgment continues then in verse 17 with a picture of flight (*tānusû*) in an utter rout.[46] It concludes with a final play on the key word *nûs*. The disaster and rout are so great that all that remains is a sign (*nēs*) of their having been there.

[44] On the covenantal context of *'abāh* see the discussion of 1:19–20 and the references cited there.

[45] Polarity of meaning in Hebrew verbs is a well-known phenomenon, e.g. *yaraš* = "possess" and "dispossess", but such polarity is usually demonstrated by several examples rather than one.

[46] Note that the punishment here is a reverse adaptation of the covenant blessing in Lev 26:8

"Five of you shall pursue a hundred and a hundred of you shall pursue ten thousand; and your enemies shall fall before you by the sword."

In a careful stylistic interaction of catchword, paranomasia, and simile the prophet proclaims a judgment speech whose meaning is clear and its irony inescapable. The sin and the judgment can be summed up in one word *nûs*. The sin leads to the judgment and the judgment correlates with the sin. The punishment must be understood as Yahweh's judgment; yet the oracle itself indicates a continuity between sin and punishment so that Judah's sin brings about consequences that become her judgment. Her reliance on military action will lead to military disaster.

Isaiah 31:1–3

(1) Woe, the ones going down to Egypt for help
    (and) relying on horses,
  who trust in chariotry because they are many,
    and in horsemen because they are very numerous,
  but do not look to the Holy One of Israel
    and do not seek Yahweh.
(2) Yet he is wise and has brought disaster (*rāʿ*)
    and has not taken back his words.
  He shall rise up against the house of the evil-doers (*mērā ʿîm*)
    and against the *help* of the workers of iniquity.
(3) The Egyptians are human and not God,
    their horses flesh and not spirit.
  When Yahweh stretches out his hand,
    the *helper* shall stumble,
      and the one who is *helped* shall fall,
    and they shall all perish together.

Once again we encounter the correspondence pattern in a judgment speech that has grown out of a woe saying.[47] The initial governing description of the sin of the people is: *hôy hayyōr^{e}dîm misrayim l^{e}ʿezrāh*. That sin is spelled out in parallel expressions that indicate the same character of sin as in other Isaianic passages; trust in the military power gained by alliances rather than in Yahweh. Verse 2 then gives the announcement of punishment for the crime described in verse 1. The intended result of the crime—help (*ʿezrāh*)—is frustrated as Yahweh rises against, i.e. does battle with, the *help* Israel sought. The object of the action in the sin is also the object of Yahweh's judging action. That the prophet

[47] Janzen, *Mourning Cry and Woe Oracle*, does not list this woe-saying in his catalog of woe-sayings that include reversal of imagery (correspondence). He cites B. Childs (*Isaiah and the Assyrian Crisis* [London: SCM Press, 1967], 33–35) and Donner, *Israel unter den Völker*, 135ff. as basis for excising v 2 as an interpolation. Admitting the problem of the tenses, I am nevertheless not inclined to follow that conclusion. To eliminate verse 2 is to eliminate one of the principle points of correspondence, and verse 3 confirms that correspondence is intended. Childs says the parallel of doers of iniquity and evil-doers is confined largely to the Psalms, but Micah 2:1–5 gives us a comparable parallelism and one that, like Isaiah 31:1–3, involves the correspondence of *raʿ* and *raʿ*. Once again, awareness of the correspondence pattern may suggest a literary critical caution.

intends to make this correspondence is indicated further in the conclusion to the announcement of punishment (3bc): When Yahweh acts, helper (*ʿōzēr*) and helped one (*ʿāzur*) will fall and perish.[48] The irony exists in that Judah's action to secure her position leads her into a situation where instead she falls. That is not stated as an inevitable consequence of turning to Egypt. As far as the passage is concerned Egypt may be presumed to be a strong power—but not stronger than God. The failure of Egypt to provide the necessary help is because "Yahweh stretches out his hand." The correspondence, therefore, cannot be seen in this instance as intending to show how the consequence grows out of the deed. It is there primarily, as in other cases, to show what is at issue, what is at stake in Judah's action and Yahweh's response. The question is clearly one of *help*. Where and how does Judah find it? She has known the answer to that question throughout her history. The Psalms are replete with declarations that Yahweh is Israel's helper, that from him alone comes help from all her enemies (Pss 20:2; 22:20; 33:20; 38:23; 40:14; 44:27; 63:8; 70:2; 71:12; 94:17; 108:13; 121:1, 2; 124:8, 35c). When she turns elsewhere for help that is rebellion against Yahweh, and he will turn her expected help into disaster. The correspondence here as in 28:14ff. points to an issue that is a kind of *status confessionis* for the people.

The correspondence pattern is manifest further in a more general way but one that is found in several other places. This is in the double use of the root *rāʿaʿ* in nominal and verbal forms in verse 2. The temporal aspect of the verbs in 2a is subject to some debate but the correlation is present. Those who do *rāʿ* (evil) will encounter *rāʿ* (disaster) from the Lord. *Rāʿ* brings *rāʿ*, but not inherently. It is because Yahweh decides to meet *rāʿ* with *rāʿ*.

Isaiah 33:1

> Woe, you destroyer (*šôdēd*), who yourself have not been
> destroyed; (*lōʾ šādûd*)
> You treacherous one (*bōgēd*) with whom none has
> dealt treacherously (*lōʾ bāg^{e}dû bô*).
> When you have completed destroying (*šôdēd*), you shall be
> destroyed (*tûšad*);
> when you have finished dealing treacherously (*libgōd*),
> you shall be dealt with treacherously (*yibg^{e}dû bāk*).

This verse is a woe-saying judgment speech that serves to introduce the complex block of material that is Chapter 33. The chapter is probably of a later date than Isaiah, but its historical locus is difficult to uncover. Verse 1 stands somewhat apart from the rest of the chapter. It is a unit in itself with an indictment and announcement of punishment, and it is followed by an entreaty in direct address to Yahweh.

[48] For MT *w^{e}lōʾ rûaḥ* LXX has *ouk esti boētheia*, apparently reading *w^{e}lōʾ ʿezrāh*.

The correspondence between sin and punishment in this case requires little comment inasmuch as it is very obvious and repetitive. Indeed that is the most noticeable thing about the verse. It builds on a parallelism and repetition that appears in Isaiah 21:2 (*habbôgēd bôgēd w*[e]*haššôdēd šôdēd*). In the latter passage the short almost staccato passage combines alliteration and end-rhyme to produce a pointed and potent bicolon. The verse above uses these same verbs (*šādad* and *bāgad*) in an extreme form of correspondence that appears to represent a kind of baroque development of a rhetorical device, the power of which is somewhat lessened by the fact that the correspondence is overdone, each of the corresponding verbs being used four times in one verse.

The correlation is there, however, and one cannot miss it. It is talionic in character indicating that what the accused has done will be done to him. Like Hab 2:16 (see below) the passage indicates that the destroyer will eventually have his turn and the cup he has made others drink will come round at last to him. It implies a period of uninterrupted destruction and treachery (i.e. "You yourself have not been destroyed . . . when you have completed destroying") in which a reign of terror is carried out by someone without cause. That will run its course and then the judgment will come, inflicting upon the sinner the same terror he has inflicted upon others. No details of how this will happen, the character of the action, or the agent administering it are given. The judgment may or may not be set loose in the sinful deed—but it will come, somehow, in like fashion to the sin itself.

The Prophets of the Seventh–Sixth Centuries

In the seventh–sixth centuries the correspondence of sin and punishment is found in several examples from Habakkuk and Jeremiah as well as Ezekiel, though neither of these last two prophets appears to have used this mode of prophetic speech as widely as his predecessor, Isaiah of Jerusalem. Some of the texts, however, that are discussed in the following pages manifest the complexity and diversity that are found in the way earlier prophets correlated crime and punishment. In a few cases here, as in the prophecy of Isaiah, failure to pay attention to this dimension of the prophetic rhetoric has led to unnecessary emendations or critical surgery on the text.

Habakkuk 2:6b–8a

(6b) Woe, the one heaping up what is not his own—
how long?
and loading upon himself pledges.
(7) Will not your biters/debtors suddenly rise up
and those who make you tremble awake?
Then you will be booty for them.
(8) Because *you* have *plundered* many nations,
all the rest of the peoples will *plunder* you
for human blood and violence to the earth,
the city and all its inhabitants.

The reference to the nations suggests that the passage has in mind a foreign leader of some sort. The crime is described as one of accumulating what does not belong to one and taking pledges. If that refers to the action of a nation or a king, then presumably booty and tribute are meant. Verses 7c–8a confirm that conclusion and identify the fundamental sin under judgment in these verses as the sin of plundering other nations. The appropriate punishment for the plunderer is to be plundered. So the woe oracle becomes a judgment speech announcing that poetic justice. The correspondence is elaborated freely in verses 6b–7 where the plundering activity is described in 6b in terms of taking what does not belong to one or loading up with pledges—money and tribute exacted—and the punishment in 7b. You will be booty for them (i.e. those from whom you have taken booty). The correspondence is made literal and explicit then in the climactic verse 8a:

Indictment: *You* have *plundered* (*šallôtā*) *nations* (*gôyīm*).
Punishment: People (*ʿammîn*) will *plunder* (*y*ᵉ*šallû*) *you*.

The situation will be reversed and what this ruler has done to others they will do to him. In the processes of history talion will be carried out against the plundering ruler.

By using the language of pledges for the tribute or booty of the nations, the oracle suggests that the peoples are debtors awaiting the return of the pledges, that is, that the deed by its nature will surely lead to the consequence described here. One notes, further, that there is no reference to divine agency here (Yahweh's control of the punishment is, however, indicated in the next example from this passage, vv 15–17). It is an instance of *Tun-Ergehen*, the fateful deed working out its own consequences.

Habakkuk 2:15–16

(15) Woe to the one who causes his neighbor to drink
from the goblet[1] of your[2] wrath, indeed
become drunk to gaze on their nakedness!
(16) You have become sated with disgrace instead of honor.
Drink, yourself, and show yourself uncircumcised.
The cup in the right hand of the Lord will come round to you;
and disgrace will be upon your honor.[3]

These verses are not without their problems of text and meaning, but they provide another case of a woe oracle in the context of a judgment speech where the judgment corresponds in a rather detailed way to the sin. The judgment is directed against a political power, presumably the Chaldaeans, though that cannot be determined definitely and some have seen this attack directed against the Judaean king.

The judgment speech is created out of the metaphor of drunkenness. The accused is indicted for having caused his neighbor to have drunk so much from the cup of his wrath that he has become drunk and exposed his nakedness (cf. Gen 9:21). In other words the crime of the accused king/nation is that he has so overwhelmed another nation with his power and might, his anger, that the other nation has been put to shame and disgrace before the world. The actual deed or deeds against the other nation(s) are not indicated. But the indictment points to a mode of politics and international relations where one nation pours out its might intemperately against another or others so that they become weak and dishonored.

[1] Assuming a dittography of *ḥet* and redistributing the consonants to read *missap ḥ^{a}māt^{e}kā* (cf. *sap ra'al* in Zech 12:2), the MT would be translated "joining to your wrath."

[2] 1QHab has "his wrath."

[3] Verse 17 has been omitted from the discussion because there is considerable uncertainty about its proper locus, as a glance at the commentaries reveals. If it is in its proper location after v 16, then it would belong to this unit and serve to develop further the punishment announced in v 16.

The function of the first colon of verse 16 is a matter of debate. Ward[4] and Nowack[5] would omit this colon or move it to the end of verse 16 where it seems to fit better. But the colon is in its proper place and needs to be seen as part of the description of sin or indictment, a conclusion that can be reached on other grounds but is confirmed by attention to the element of correspondence in the passage. The major shift in the passage takes place between the first and second colon of verse 16 with the imperative address to the accused (*šᵉteh*!). At the beginning of the announcement of judgment the imperative is perfectly clear and appropriate. If the preceding colon is regarded as the beginning of the judgment speech, then the imperative "Drink" is puzzling after a prior announcement of satiation and the first colon as a judgment word appears to belong better with the end of the verse. Indeed it is that assumption that 16a is part of the judgment that leads Ward and Nowack to move it.[6] One notes further that the perfect tense or *qatal* form of *śāba'* should be translated in this context with a perfect sense, as is true of other *qatal* forms in this passage (e.g. vv 8,10,18), rather than a future sense, which is regularly conveyed here with imperfect or *yiqtol* forms. The continuation of the woe oracle with a further second person address that continues the indictment and in a sense reiterates it is not unusual in a woe oracle-judgment speech as one may see from the function of verse 11a in the judgment speech of Amos 5:7, 10–11.

The indictment for crimes contains, therefore, three basic elements:

(a) making a neighbor drink wrath till drunk of it;
(b) consequent exposure of the neighbor's nakedness;
(c) becoming satiated with dishonor or disgrace (wrought upon one's neighbor) rather than honor (rendered to one's neighbor).

Examination of the judgment speech that begins in 16a leads to the recognition that the judgment or punishment corresponds to the crime at all three points, a fact that has been little noted and has exercised little control over some of the many emendations proposed in these verses.

(a) The one who makes his neighbor drink (*mašqeh*) from the goblet of his wrath will himself (*'attāh*) drink from the cup of Yahweh's right hand. The right hand of Yahweh is the Lord's might and power that finds and destroys his enemies. The "cup of Yahweh's right hand" thus corresponds to "the goblet of your wrath." The accused will have to drink from the same sort of cup from which he has made others drink.
(b) The verb *hē'ārēl* in v 16 is frequently emended to *hērā'ēl* (RSV "and stagger").[7] The presence of similar images of drinking Yahweh's wrath and staggering (e.g. Isa 51:17,22) and the simple metathesis required for emendation make this an

[4] Ward, ICC, 17.

[5] Nowack, HKAT, 264.

[6] "The omission of the first clause is required, as it anticipates the cause of the shame in the next two members, and repeats the last member" (Ward, ICC, 17).

[7] The emendation is supported by 1QHab and LXX.

appealing suggestion. But such a move destroys the correspondence between sin and punishment that is carefully worked out here and continues in the verb *hēʿārēl*. The denominative appears one other time in the Qal. The Niphal form in this passage must mean: "be counted as uncircumcised" or "show yourself uncircumcised," which Ward has properly interpreted as "implying the double shame of personal exposure and also uncircumcision."[8] As the action of the accused is making others drink so that their nakedness will be exposed to their shame, so his drinking will lead to the shameful exposure of his nakedness.

(c) Finally, the apparently misplaced v 16a: "You have become sated with disgrace (*qālôn*) instead of honor, (*kābôd*)" is balanced perfectly by the consequent fate of the accused upon whose former honor (*kābôd*) there will be heaped up disgrace (*qîqalôn*).

The symmetry of sin and judgment, the divine poetic justice, is thus announced in detail by the judgment speech of the prophet. All that the accused has done will be done to him in every respect. A metaphor to describe sin becomes an equally powerful medium to announce an appropriate punishment. The judgment will come by the hand of Yahweh—literally, according to the passage. The picture is one of a future but inexorably moving fate. Yahweh has made his people drink from the cup of his wrath, indeed, apparently at the hand of the one accused in this passage. But eventually the cup which the accused has put to the lips of others will come round the table for him to drink also.

Jeremiah 5:12–17

One of the more complex examples of correspondence is found in these verses from Jeremiah, a passage where the definition and delimitation of the unit is no small problem and the subject of some disagreement among commentators. The recognition of the stylistic technique under consideration here may, however, help resolve the question of the limits of the units or sub-units.

Bright regards vv 10–19 as a complex made up of 10–14, 15–17, and 18–19, the last an editorial prose conclusion presumably of Exilic date.[9] We may eliminate 18–19 from consideration and look at vv 10–17. R. Bach has properly seen in vv 10–11 one of the frequent calls to battle that appear in the prophetic oracles, imperatives issuing commands to fight or to flee battle (cf. Jer 6:1ff.).[10] Verse 10 issues the command to go up and destroy Judah and verse 11 gives the reason why, followed by *n^{e}'um yahweh*. This would seem to be the initial unit of the complex with what follows spelling out the details of the general indictment in v 11. Then the question remains as to whether vv 12–17 are one or two units. The rationale for separating 12–14

[8] Ward, ICC.

[9] J. Bright, *Jeremiah* (Garden City, N.J.: Doubleday and Company, 1965) 42.

[10] R. Bach, *Die Aufforderungen zur Flucht und zum Kampf im alttestamentlichen Prophetenspruch* (WMANT, 9; Neukirchen-Vluyn: Neukirchener Verlag, 1962) 59.

and 15–17 is clear. Verses 12–14 comprise a characteristic judgment speech with indictment in verses 12–13 and announcement of judgment in verse 14. They have to do with the prophetic word, and the correspondence stylistic technique can be seen within this judgment speech. Verses 15–17 then have to do with an announcement of judgment accomplished by Yahweh through the agency of another nation. This division corresponds basically to the change in person from third person reference to Judah in vv 12–14 to second person in vv 15–17.

Such a division is quite plausible and may be the correct one. I would like to suggest, however, that 12–17 may be a whole unit with a complex correspondence between the elements of the indictment in vv 12–13 and the elements of the announcement of judgment in vv 14–17. For one thing, the shift in person between 14 and 15 is not as neat as it seems at first. In vv 12–14 the people are generally spoken of in third person. An exception to this, however, appears in the *dabberkem* of v 14 which is regularly emended to *dabb^e^rām* to make it agree with the third person of v 12 and distinguish it from the second person singular address to the prophet in verse 14b. The conjecture may be correct. Certainly a second person address to two distinct addresses in the same verse is strange and awkward. Awkward though it may be, however, the MT at this point should not be dismissed too quickly. The proposed emendation is conjectural and without textual basis. The singular and plural second persons in this verse allow a distinction to be made: "Because *you* (the people) have done so and so, I am going to do this with *you* (the prophet)." Further in v 19 we are confronted with exactly the same phenomenon again: In the same sentence Yahweh addresses the people in second person plural and the prophet in second person singular. Here, also, of course, some sort of emendation is usually made.

When all of this is taken into consideration, therefore, one may not easily speak of a shift of persons between verses 14 and 15. The "you" (pl.) of v 15 may be anticipated in the "you" (pl.) of v 14.

One other textual problem needs to be looked at. The conclusion of verse 13 reads: "Thus shall it be done to them" [*kōh yêʿāśeh lāhem*]. As Bright notes in his commentary, this clause fits poorly here and indeed is omitted in LXX^{A}. Bright suggests with Duhm, Rudolph, and others (cf. MT critical note) that the clause may have fallen out of verse 14. He restores it to v 14 and translates:

> Because they (MT—you) have uttered this word,
> Thus will it be done to them.

Such a transposition only makes good sense if the "you" of the *yaʿan* clause is emended to "they." It does make better sense of the whole if v 13 is understood as a continuation of the people's remarks in v 12. Bright argues, however, that v 13 is Jeremiah's rejoinder about the false prophets who are responsible for the sentiments expressed in v 12 (cf. 14:13f.). That fits the context since the preceding words are clearly indebted to the prophets. Further, in Jeremiah "the prophets" regularly is Jeremiah's designation of the contemporary prophets, not a designation by the people of prophets like Jeremiah. The principal problem for this interpretation is the fact that it seems to anticipate the word of judgment that begins properly in v 14. The correspondence between sin and judgment is present whether v 13 contains the words of Jeremiah or of the people. An even greater correspondence exists if v 13 comes from the people as an attack on true prophets.

The indictment that is leveled against Judah, i.e. their sin or crime, is that they have said something about Yahweh, something false. That is, the crime is not an unjust deed, an act of apostasy. It is a word spoken about Yahweh. So in the judgment announced it is made immediately clear that the punishment will be a word spoken to and about them by Yahweh:

> "Because you [they?] have spoken this word,
> behold I am putting my words in
> your [sing.] mouth for a fire.

Corresponding to the word of sin will be a word of judgment, a word that is a devouring fire.

But the correspondence goes even further if vv 15–17 are recognized as a part of the announcement of judgment. The false word that is a sin is the claim that Yahweh will do nothing to them, a claim expressed in two ways:

> No evil shall come upon us; [*wᵉlōʾ tābôʾ ʿālênû rāʿāh*]
> nor will we see sword or famine.

The first claim receives a word of judgment corresponding to it in v 15:

> Behold I am bringing upon you a nation from afar
> [*hinᵉnî mēbîʾ ʿᵃlêkem goy mimmerḥaq*].

Their sin is the claim that no evil will come upon them. If this is a sin, then the appropriate judgment is that Yahweh will bring evil upon them—in the form of a foreign nation. Then the second claim, which is that they will not see sword or famine, is responded to with an announcement that they will see both sword (v 17c) and famine (v 17ab). A further link between 12–14 and 15–17 is found in the word *ʾākal*, which is the verb expressing the judgment in v 14 and in v 17 where it is repeated four times.

If one can understand v 13 as part of the false word of the people, then the correspondence between sin and judgment goes even deeper. For their claim that the word is not in the prophets will be met by Yahweh putting his word in the mouth of Jeremiah. And the claim that the prophets are empty wind is answered by the judgment that the prophetic word will become a devouring fire.

Finally we note, as in most of the other cases, that the technique of formulating a judgment corresponding to the sin does not produce a notion of judgment that is extraordinary or trivial. On the contrary, the prophetic word of Yahweh did consume the people, and their judgment came at the hands of a distant nation (Yahweh's *rā'āh* upon the people) who brought famine and sword. And while the judgment that ensues arises in part out of the sinful actions of the people, the correspondence described by the prophets is not one of a fate-effecting deed but one wrought out by the action of Yahweh, which the prophet perceives to be directed toward a particular sin and therefore appropriate punishment.

Jeremiah 5:19

> When you say, "Why has Yahweh our God done all these things to us?" you shall say to them, "As you have abandoned me and served foreign gods in your land, so shall you serve strangers in a land which is not yours."

The character of the correspondence in this case is sufficiently clear that it needs little elaboration. It nevertheless is succinct and forceful as it announces a punishment markedly like the sin which has led to it. The change of address from the people to Jeremiah in the same sentence is similar to v 14, as was noted in the discussion of that verse. The intention of comparing the sin and the judgment is indicated by the *ka'^{a}šer . . . kēn* sequence, and the comparison itself centers in the repetition of the verb "serve" (*'ābad*). The "as . . . so" sequence reminds one of the *lex talionis* formulation in Leviticus (see below) but the formulation is not the same. The sin of serving strange gods brings on the punishment of serving a strange or foreign people. The correlation is fairly extensive although it does not involve precise repetition of every word. The verb *'āzab* in the indictment could have been used appropriately in the announcement of punishment but was not. But the rest of the indictment is matched in detail in the judgment announcement. The verb (*ta'ab^{e}dû*) is repeated. The *zārîm* whom they will serve correspond to the *'^{e}lōhê nēkār* whom they will serve, and a pointed poetic justice is created as the service of strange gods leads to the service of strangers. The adverbial phrase *b^{e}'arṣ^{e}kem* indicating location "in your land" in the indictment is quite intentional. It is matched by the judgment of serving strangers "in a land that is not yours (*b^{e}'ereṣ lō' lākem*). The judgment speech neatly turns the sin of worship of other gods to provide security and fertility for Judah's land into the punishment of foreign subjugation in exile. But the process of doing that sharply connects the two so that the relationship of the one to the other cannot be missed.

Jeremiah 14:13–16

A passage that is in many ways quite similar to 5:12–17 is Jer 14:13–16. The indictment is given by Jeremiah and Yahweh in verses 13–14. Formally the indictment is Yahweh's accusation that the prophets prophesy lies in his name. The specific lie that they prophesy is that the people will not see sword or famine. The corresponding judgment is made explicit in v 15:

> Therefore thus says the Lord concerning the prophets . . . who say, "*Sword and famine* shall not come on this land": *By sword and famine* shall those prophets be consumed.

Further:

> And the people to whom they prophesy shall be cast out in the streets of Jerusalem, *because of famine and sword* . . . (v 16).

The actuality or reality of the judgment is of course the same as Jer 5:12–17 above.

Jeremiah 23:1–2

The passage contains Jeremiah's woe oracle as judgment speech against the "shepherds" of Israel. The announcement of judgment is expressed entirely in terms of correspondence that involves both the use of the same verb in stating the action of the sin and the action of punishment and a play on words. It may be seen in the words italicized.

Indictment for sin:

> Alas, the shepherds (*rōʿîm*) destroying and scattering the flock of my pasture (*marʿîtî*)!—oracle of Yahweh—Therefore, thus says Yahweh, God of Israel, against/concerning the *shepherds shepherding* (*hārōʿîm hārōʿîm*) my people: *You* have scattered them, that is my flock, and driven them away and have not *tended* (*pᵉqadtem*) to them.

Announcement of punishment:

> So I will *tend* (*hinᵉnî pōqēd*) to you for the *evil* (*rōaʿ*) of your deeds.

The indictment expresses the sin of the people in various ways. The last characterization (*lō* + *pāqad*) becomes the point of correspondence. Failure to *pāqad* means that you will suffer *pāqad*. The verb has, therefore, in successive uses positive and negative meanings. Because the shepherds did not *pāqad* the people in a positive way, Yahweh will *pāqad* the shepherds in a negative way.

But the correspondence is carried further. It involves not just repetition of the central term but a play on words with the base *rōʿ*-. There are three references to the leaders as *rōʿîm* (plus a reference to Yahweh's *marʿîtî*). Corresponding to that is the identification of their deeds which bring judgment as *rōaʿ*. The *rōʿîm* have done *roaʿ*. While the *rōaʿ* refers to the sin, it appears in the punishment section thus carrying the correspondence by wordplay.

The use of *pāqad* and *rāʿah* as the thematic words and the vehicles of correlation is carried over into the salvation words of verse 4. Yahweh will set up shepherds (*rōʿîm*) who will do the proper shepherding task (*wᵉrāʿûm*) and this time they will all be tended to, accounted for, i.e., none will be missing (*lō' yippāqēdû*). In a similar manner to some of Isaiah's oracles the correlation of crime and punishment is extended to a consequent deliverance.

Jeremiah 30:16

> Therefore all who devour you (*'ōkᵉlayik*) shall be
> devoured (*yē'ākēlû*)
> and all your adversaries, every one of them,
> shall go into captivity.
> Those who plunder you (*šō'sayik*) shall become
> plunder (*mᵉšissāh*);
> and all who prey on you (*bōzᵉzayik*) I will
> make into prey (*baz*).

In this part of Jeremiah, commonly known as "The Book of Consolation," 30:12–17 describes in detail the incurable wound which Judah has received from Yahweh because of the extent of her sin and guilt. This rather detailed diagnosis of a hopeless and terminal case turns into a promise of healing in the final two verses as the prophet announces judgment against Judah's oppressors. That announcement is expressed almost entirely by means of the correspondence pattern using repetition of words. The healing of Judah and the judgment of her enemies happens as they undergo the fate they brought upon Judah. Three out of the four cola characterize the punishment this way (*'okᵉlayik-yē'ākēlû*; *šō'sayik-mᵉšissāh*; *bōzᵉzayik→baz*), and if one acknowledges the context of the whole Book of Jeremiah and particularly chapters 30–31, it is self-evident that the judgment of exile upon Judah's enemies is also meant to correlate with the exile inflicted upon her. The formulation is quite talionic in its meaning and comes close to being that in its style, especially v 16a (see last chapter). The intent and content of this verse are quite similar to Isa 33:1, although the two passages use different words to characterize the sin and punishment. Jeremiah 30:16 does not characterize the actions of Judah's enemies as sin. Indeed, it is clear that they have been Yahweh's agents to deal with Judah's sin. But as so often in the prophets, Israel's or Judah's enemies are not under some kind of divine immunity for the oppression even though Yahweh has made that oppression his instrument. They, too, are accountable for the wounds they inflict, and the moment of accountability will be Judah's healing.

Ezekiel 27–28

The *qinah* or lament that is raised against Tyre in Ezek 27 is formulated around an extended metaphor of the city as a magnificent ship decked out in splendor derived from her commercial activities with neighbors far and near. The metaphor, singularly appropriate for the city of Tyre, is broken up into two parts. The first section (vv 3b–9) describes the glory of the ship as a device for characterizing the past greatness of Tyre. After a prosaic insertion (11–25a) which relinquishes the metaphor to describe in catalogue fashion the various articles of trade and merchandise between Tyre and other localities, the lament of the ship picks up again, probably in 25b, with the second part. The break in the lament coincides with the movement from description of past greatness as a reflection of the pride of Tyre to present or imminent destruction of this great ship (vv 25b/26–36).[11]

The metaphor derives from Tyre's important location as a great seaport. Because Tyre was in fact located "in" the sea and the sea(s) formed the foundation of greatness, the use of the imagery of the ship serves to underscore the significance of the sea for Tyre's existence, indicating in the first part the sea as the locale and source of her splendor and in the second the sea as the context or locale of her destruction. The theme and vocabulary of the sea serves, therefore, to create a correlation between the past pride of Tyre and the doom that has come upon her.

This thematic correspondence is carried primarily though not exclusively by the phrase *b^e^leb yammin*, which appears four times in chapter 27 and twice in chapter 28, the judgment against the prince of Tyre. Tyre is characterized in the introduction as "the one who dwells at the entrance to the sea" (MT *hayyōšebet ʿal-m^e^bôʾōt yām*—probably to be corrected to *hayyōšebet ʿal-m^e^bôʾ hayyām*).[12] Then at the beginning of the description (27:4), the second line of the direct address to Tyre, the text reads *b^e^lēb yammîm g^e^bûlayik*, "Your borders are in the midst of the seas," i.e. the ship of Tyre is set in the sea, indeed at the entrance to the sea. That locale, however, which enabled the rise of Tyre to greatness, becomes the place of her destruction in the lament that continues in 27:25ff. Verse 25b is a transitional line:

> *wattimāl^e^ʾî wattikb^e^dî m^e^ʾōd*
> *b^e^lēb yammîm*
> You became full and heavily laden
> in the midst of the seas.

The sentence serves in part to describe Tyre's great wealth acquired by her maritime activity and in part to forecast the destruction that has come to the heavily laden ship caught "in the midst of the seas."[13] That doom in and by

[11] For a detailed literary analysis along these lines see W. Zimmerli, *Ezechiel 25–48*, (BKAT XI11/2; Neukirchen-Vluyn: Neukirchener Verlag, 1969) 634–38. Cf. the same work, 600–606, for discussion of the historical context of these chapters.

[12] *Ibid.*, 626.

[13] Zimmerli's objections to the originality of 25b are not fully convincing. They are as follows:

(a) The merchandise suggested by the picture of the full ship refers back to the goods of vv 12–24.

(b) The final two words of 25b anticipate very unattractively (*sehr unschön*) the concluding words of v 26. (This judgment is also rendered against the same two words in v 27, which Zimmerli sees as an *unschöne Wiederholung* of the expression in v 26.)

the sea is then described in vv 26ff. Her rowers have brought the ship of Tyre into the *mayim rabbîm* (26a). "The east wind (has) wrecked you in the midst of the seas (*bᵉlēb yammîm*)." Verse 27 describes the extent or totality of the ship's destruction by listing its contents, passengers, and crew with the concluding words:

> *yippᵉlû bᵉlēb yammîm*
> *bᵉyôm mappaltēk*
> They fall into the midst of the seas
> on the day of your fall.

Once again the prophetic word pointedly locates the fall of Tyre in the same place as her rise and her glory—in the midst of the seas. The remaining verses make no further allusion to *lēb yammîm*, but they reiterate the role of the sea as the source of Tyre's ruin:

> (32) *mî kᵉṣôr nidmāh* (MT *kᵉdûmāh*)[14]
> *bᵉtôk hayyām*
> Who was ever (destroyed)[15] like Tyre
> in the midst of the sea?

> (34) *'attā* (MT *'ēt*)[16] *nišberet miyyammîm*
> *bᵉma'ᵃmaqqê mayim*
> Now you are wrecked by the seas,
> in the depths of the waters.

The judgment speech against the prince of Tyre in chapter 28 also uses the phrase *bᵉlēb yammîm* as a device for correlating the indictment and the announcement of judgment:

With regard to the first of Zimmerli's objections, the line is completely consistent with the imagery of the ship and may be the basis for the insertion of 12–24/25a at this point. The second and third objections depend too heavily on subjective aesthetic judgments. The absence of a corresponding five-beat line does not in itself betray a secondary insertion at all, and indeed Zimmerli has to assume the same thing for an earlier line (8b) to maintain the sequence of pairs. As for the unattractive anticipation and repetition of the words *bᵉlēb yammîm*, it is precisely the opposite that is the case when the verses are looked at with the prophetic correspondence motif in mind. The phrase *bᵉlēb yammîm* appears only one other time (Ps 46:3) outside of these chapters. It occurs *six* times in chapters 27 and 28. In both chapters it is a repetitive device for the correspondence of sin and judgment although 27:3b–9 is, as Zimmerli notes, quite unpolemical in its form and does not elaborate the splendor of Tyre in strong tones of indictment and accusation (see below). Rather than being *unschön* the repetition of *bᵉlēb yammîm* stylistically carries much of the weight for creating the correlation.

[14] Following Zimmerli's analysis and emendation of the text, *Ezechiel*, 633.

[15] The homonymy of *dāmāh* I, "be like, resemble" and *dāmāh* II "cease, cut off, destroy" creates a definite ambiguity in the context. If the verb is *dāmāh* I, then the sentence alludes back to Tyre's previous greatness as a contrast to her present state. If the verb is *dāmāh* II, then the line is a lament for the awfulness of Tyre's "shipwreck." The text does not allow one to say with certainty which is the correct translation although the Niphal form argues in favor of *dāmāh* I.

[16] So with most of the versions. Cf. Zimmerli, *Ezechiel*, 634.

Indictment:

(2b) Because your heart is proud,
and you said: "I am God,
I dwell in the seat of the gods
in the midst of the seas (*b*^e*lēb yammîm*)."

Announcement of judgment:

(6) Therefore thus says Lord Yahweh:
"Because you consider your heart
like the heart of God,

(7) therefore I am going to bring strangers upon you, the most terrible of the nations, and they shall draw their sword against the beauty of your wisdom and defile your splendor. They shall thrust you down into the pit, and you shall die the death of the slain in the heart of the seas (*bᵉlēb yammîm*).

Chapter 26 expresses also the judgment of God against Tyre explicitly in terms of the sea and the waters (vv 3, 5, 14, 16, 17–18, 19). When this chapter with its strong judgment speech character is placed before chapter 27, and chapter 28, also a judgment speech against Tyre, is placed afterward, the effect is to turn the whole sequence of chapters, including the lament that is chapter 27, into a series of judgment oracles. For chapter 27 that means that the description of Tyre in vv 1–25 serves as a kind of indictment. That may not have been the original intention of these verses if the original form of the text in v 3c was *ṣôr 'att 'ᵃnî*, "you are a ship," instead of *ṣôr 'att 'āmart'ᵃnî*, as may well have been the case.[17] But the present form of v 3, which now parallels the indictment of 28:2 (*'ēl 'ᵃnî*), in the context of chapters 26 and 28 means that 27:1ff. must be seen as a description of Tyre's crime, and 27:26 (v 25b is transitional) is a lament that now announces the punishment.

The end result is a prophetic correlation of sin and punishment that is intricate and arises in part out of the history of transmission of the text. The correspondence is created out of the motif of the sea, which was central to the history and existence of Tyre. It is reinforced and emphasized by the repetition of the words *bᵉlēb yammîm*. The punishment relates to the crime sharply also by focusing on the instrument of Tyre's sin. While the initial indictment speaks of Tyre's rejoicing because of Jerusalem's misfortune (26:2), chapters 27 and 28 clearly identify Tyre's sin as inordinate pride because of her position, a place of pre-eminence created by her location in the sea and her mastery of maritime commerce. The judgment of Yahweh, however, is that she who lived by the sea will fall by or into the sea. The means of her pride becomes the means of her destruction.

[17] See the text critical discussion in Zimmerli, *Ezechiel*, 626–27.

Ezekiel 15:14–15

(14) Thus says the Lord Yahweh:
"As (you) rejoiced that all the land is desolate (*š^e^māmāh*) (so) I will do it to you.
(15) As you rejoiced over the inheritance of the house of Israel because it has become desolate (*šāmēmāh*), so I will do to you. You shall become desolate (*š^e^māmāh tihyeh*), Mount Seir, and all Edom, all of it. Then they shall know that I am Yahweh."[18]

Despite the corruption of the text, it is easily seen that the prophetic oracle centers upon the repetition of nominal and verbal forms of the root *šmm*. Edom's crime is to see the desolation of the house of Israel as an opportunity for her to take over land and territory that belonged to her ancient rival. The logic of such an assumption from Edom's point of view is inescapable. But it ignores the reality declared by the prophet that the fate of the house of Israel is a part of Yahweh's purposes and not for the sake of Edom's aggrandizement. All of chapters 36–37 denounce the intention of Edom and others to capitalize on Israel's misfortune. To do so would be to move against the intention of Yahweh to re-establish the house of Israel on this land after she has undergone judgment. Edom's judgment is not intrinsically an outgrowth of her crime; but Yahweh will bring about a poetic judgment. The desolation (*š^e^māmāh*) which was the occasion of her sin as it was experienced by Judah will become her own fate as Yahweh's judgment.

The centrality of *š^e^māmāh* as the organizing motif of the oracle against Edom is indicated both by the conclusion of the chapter in this judgment speech about *š^e^māmāh* and by the anticipation of the theme in vv 3–4, where the root *šmm* appears three times (twice as noun and once as verb, as in vv 14–15). Verse 4b very precisely forecasts the conclusion of the chapter and the whole of verses 3–4 and 14–15 provide an inclusio for the oracle against Edom. The thematic word/root is then picked up again several times in the chapter (verses 7 [2x], 9, and 12).

Ezekiel 36:6

Therefore prophesy concerning the land of Israel and say to the mountains and hills, to the ravines and valleys: "Thus says the Lord Yahweh: 'See, I speak in my jealousy and in my anger because you have suffered the reproach of nations (*k^e^limmat gôyim n^e^śā'tem*).' Therefore thus says the Lord Yahweh: 'I lift up my hand in oath (*'^a^nî nāśā'tî 'et – yādî*): truly the nations that are round about you, they themselves shall suffer reproach'" (*hēmmāh k^e^limmātām yiśśā'û*).

[18] The text clearly seems to be corrupt in v 14. The translation attempts to make sense out of the text without being certain of its original form. Verse 15a may be a gloss or a variant form of v 14 which has come into the text. See the text critical discussion in Zimmerli, *Ezechiel*, 853 and in W. Eichrodt, *Ezekiel* (Philadelphia: Westminster, 1970), 485.

The correlation here is obvious and similar to the one just described in 35:14–15. That is not surprising in light of the integral relationship of the two chapters. Here again judgment comes to foreign nations because of their attitude toward Israel. What the nations have done to Israel (*nāśā' kᵉlimmāh*) is a common one in Ezekiel (16:52, 54; 32:24ff., 30; 34:29; 39:26; 44:13), but this is the only place where it is used in this way within a formal judgment speech. There may even be an intended emphasis of the correspondence by the use of *nāśā'* in the oath formula, though that is difficult to say because here too we have a familiar expression in Ezekiel (20:5f.,15,23, 28,42; 42; 44:12) which in one other instance (44:12) appears in association with *nāśā' kᵉlimmāh*. The character of the judgment speech if not the form is clearly talionic (see below).[19]

[19] So also Eichrodt, *Ezekiel*, 491.

Other Poetic Texts

Two other passages of a prophetic character are worth noting before turning to the narrative corpus. They are Joel 3:4–8 and Deut 32:21. Both of these texts are detailed and almost paradigmatic examples of the correlation of sin and punishment.

Joel 3:4–8[1]

(4) What are you to me, Tyre and Sidon,
and all the districts of Philistia?
Are you paying me back,
Or are you doing something to me?
Swiftly and speedily I will bring back your
deed upon your own head.
(5) Because you took my silver and my gold,
and carried my rich treasures into your palaces,
(6) and the people of Judah and the people of Jerusalem
you sold to the Greeks
so as to remove them far from their territory,
(7) Now I am going to rouse them up from the place
to which you sold them,
and I will bring your deed back upon
your own head,
(8) I will sell your sons and daughters
into the hand of the people of Judah
and they shall sell them to Sabaeans,
to a far off nation;
For Yahweh has spoken.

The judgment speech begins in v 4 with a general statement of the correspondence pattern. Their sinful deed will be brought back upon them (see final chapter). Then the *indictment* is given in vv 5–6. It has two parts to it:

(a) You took my silver, gold, and treasures into
your palaces
(b) You sold (*m^ekartem*) the people of Judah and
Jerusalem to Greece, to send them far off
(*l^ema'an harḥîqām*).

[1] Some regard these verses as prose, but prosodic characteristics are clearly present as recognized for example, by BHS and H. W. Wolff, *Joel and Amos*, (Hermeneia; Philadelphia: Fortress Press, 1977) 72.

The *announcement* of *punishment* comes in vv 7–8. It reiterates the general statement of correspondence.[2] Then it turns to the specifics of the indictment, ignoring the first part of it while providing a detailed correlation of the punishment with the second part of the indictment. Poetic justice is expressed first of all in the fact that the victims of their crime become the agents of their punishment and secondly in the exact duplication of their deed in their punishment. The correlation can be expressed as follows:

Crime:	A sells B to C, a far-off place.
Punishment:	B sells A to D, a far-off nation.

The correlation is not an unnatural one. In both cases the deed refers to slave trade arising out of conquest.[3] Nor is it surprising to anticipate a slave group turning the tables on those who sent them into slavery. One can perceive, therefore, signs of the *Tun-Ergehen* relationship.[4] But the action cannot be reduced to that in light of the action of Yahweh and the high degree of emphasis on correspondence rather than consequence.[5] In any case the text provides one of the clearest examples of poetic justice in the prophets.

Deut 32:21

The dating and historical locus of this Psalm remain a matter of considerable debate. Eissfeldt followed by Albright argued for a quite early eleventh century date.[6] G. E. Wright with the support of Cross has defended a ninth century date.[7] David Robertson in his dissertation on *Linguistic Evidence in the Dating of Early Hebrew Poetry* sees possible archaic elements in the poem but suggests they may be indications of archaizing.[8] More recently Freedman has supported a date in the late tenth or early ninth century.[9]

[2] The repetition of a general statement of correspondence within an elaborated specific example is not a common phenomenon.

[3] For possible historical circumstances see Wolff, *Joel and Amos*, 77–79.

[4] E.g. Wolff, *Joel and Amos*.

[5] See the discussion in the final chapter.

[6] O. Eissfeldt, *Das Lied Moses Deut, 32:1–43 und das Lehrgedicht Asaphs Psalm 78 samt einer Analyse der Ungebung des Mose-Liedes*, Berichte über die Verhandlungen der Sachsischen Akademie der Wissenschaften zu Leipzig, Philologisch—historisch Klasse, Band 104, Heft 5, 1958; and W. F. Albright, "Some Remarks on the Song of Moses in Deuteronomy XXXII," *VT* 9 (1959) 339–46.

[7] G. E. Wright, "The Lawsuit of God: A Form-Critical Study of Deuteronomy 32," *Israel's Prophetic Heritage*, ed. by B. W. Anderson and W. Harrelson (New York: Harper & Brothers, 1962), 26–67.

[8] D. A. Robertson, *Linguistic Evidence in the Dating of Early Hebrew Poetry* (SBL Dissertation Series 3; Missoula, Montana: Scholars Press, 1972), *passim.*

[9] D. N. Freedman, "Divine Names and Titles in Early Hebrew Poetry," *Magnalia Dei: The Mighty Acts of God*, ed. by F. M. Cross, W. E. Lemke, and P. D. Miller, Jr. (Garden City, N.Y.: Doubleday and Co., 1976) 79.

The precise dating of the poem is not a central concern here. The proposal of a date around the ninth century seems the most plausible alternative, but such a judgment must remain tentative. The signs of prophetic and wisdom influence (or better the presence of elements and points of view consonant with the spheres of prophecy and wisdom) make it not surprising that one should find here one of the best and most extensive examples of correspondence between sin and punishment. Indeed one may say that the central structural movement of the song hinges on that correspondence.

As Wright has demonstrated in his detailed study, Deut 32 appears to belong to the genre of the *rîb* or *lawsuit*. While others may argue with his analysis, there is no question that the poem centers upon a lengthy indictment of Israel's sin and description of the judgment that Yahweh the warrior will bring upon his people.

After the introductory call to heaven and earth and ascription of praise to Yahweh (vv 1–3), the poem begins with a summary of Yahweh's faithfulness and Israel's perversity (vv 4–6). There follows then a lengthy account of the Lord's gracious history with his people (vv 7–14) leading into a report of their rebellious and idolatrous response. The major turning point of the poem begins in v 19 and it describes Yahweh's reaction to Israel's behavior, but it centers in v 21. The verse is composed of two bicola 7 to 9 syllables per cola that manifest both internal and external parallelism. That is, the A and B cola of each line are parallel and the two lines are parallel to each other. In this intricate balance the correspondence between the nature of Israel's sin and the nature of Yahweh's judgment is laid out down to the last detail.

21a	*hēm gin'ûnî b^elō'-'ēl*	*They* have stirred me to jealous anger with what is no god;
	ki'^asûnî b^ehablêhem	they have vexed me with their idols (worthless things)
21b	*(wa)'^anî 'aqnî'ēm b^elō'-'am*	So *I* will stir them to jealously with those who are not people;
	b^egôy nābāl 'ak'îsēm	with a foolish nation I will vex them.

In 21a the basic sin of Israel against Yahweh is described. They have stirred him to jealousy (*qānā'*) or vexed (*kā'as*) him with their "no-god," (their idols) or their "worthless things" (their idols). The word *hebel* is a standard term for idol in Jeremiah (2:5, 8:19; 10:3, 8, 15 (=51:18); 14:22; 16:19) and is used also with that meaning in Dtr (1 Kgs 16:13; 22; 2 Kgs 17:15). That such a definition of Israel's sin is the crux of the matter in this poem is indicated by similar formulations in v 16 especially and v 19. Verse

16 says that "they stirred him to jealousy (*yaqni'uhû*) with strange gods (*zārîm*)" and "they vexed him (*yak'isuhû*) with abominations (*tô'ēbōt*, equivalent to *hablêhem*)." Verse 19, which begins the description of Yahweh's reaction, says that Yahweh saw this and spurned the people because of the vexation or provocation (*ka'as*) of his sons and daughters.

Then in v 21b Yahweh's judgment is announced in corresponding terms. As they have stirred him to jealousy with no god, he will stir them to jealousy with no people. They will be angry and jealous at the power and might of other nations over them. And as they have vexed Yahweh with their worthless things, their idols, so he will vex them with a foolish thing, a nation. The external parallelism to express the correspondence is, as indicated above, precise and complete.

21a (sin)
agent——independent pronoun — *hēm*
sinful action——verb — *qin'ûnî*
instrument of sin—prepositional phrase — *b*^{e}*lō' 'ēl*
sinful action——verb — *ki'*^{a}*sûnî*
instrument of sin—prepositional phrase — *b*^{e}*hablêhem*

21b (judgment)
agent——independent pronoun — *'*^{a}*nî*
judging action——verb — *'aqnî'ēm*
instrument of judgment——prepositional phrase — *b*^{e}*lō'- 'am*
judging action——verb — *'ak'isēm*
instrument of judgment——prepositional phrase — *b*^{e}*gôy nābāl*

The final element in this list, the instrument of judgment, *b*^{e}*gôy nābāl*, may not at first glance seem to be as precise an equivalent or correspondence to *b*^{e}*hablêhem* as the other element of the correspondence. But when looked at carefully it is clear that in terms of meaning and poetry it is an appropriate balance to the instrument of sin. The instrument of sin in both parts of 21a is the false god or idol. The corresponding instrument of judgment is set up in 21b as another people (*b*^{e}*lō'-'am* parallel to *b*^{e}*lō'-'ēl*. As there is one instrument of sin in this formulation, so there is one instrument of judgment, expressed in the second part of 21b by the common parallel to *'am*, i.e. *gôy*. Further, the characterization of the idols as worthless (*hebel*) is balanced by the characterization of the nation as foolish (*nābāl*). Finally one notices that poetically *b*^{e}*hablêhem* is balanced in terms of length by *b*^{e}*gôy nābāl* (4 syllables) and, even more important, *nābāl* creates a clear case of paranomasia with its corresponding term *hebel*.

So with verse 21b the poem shifts from lengthy description of sin to expanded elaboration of Yahweh's judgment. The sin, while elaborated at greater length, is given in essence in 21a. The judgment, while spelled out in powerful and mythopoeic images, is also given in a nutshell in 21b. Thus it is declared that Yahweh will match Israel's sin with divine punishment. He will deal with her in exactly the same way she has dealt with him. For a nation that has vexed its God by means of a god to whom it does not belong the appropriate punishment is for its God to vex that nation by means of a nation that does not belong to him. And the instrument of judgment is as senseless and foolish as the instrument of sin is empty and worthless. Yahweh will indeed punish Israel according to her iniquities—quite precisely with full poetic and theological justice.

Verses 22ff. build upon the summary of judgment given in 21b, a powerful declaration of the anger and destruction which Yahweh, the divine warrior, will wreak upon Israel. Typical images of judgment appear, for example, the devouring fire and pestilence. The reference to *rešep* (v 24), the picture of destruction by flame and pestilence (*rešep* and *qeteb*), and the imagery of Yahweh sending his arrows against Israel all suggest the possible influence here of the imagery and associations of the god, Rešeph, who in Canaanite mythology is called "Lord of the Arrows" (*bᶜl ḥẓ*-UT 1001:3) and appears in the theophany or epiphany of Yahweh in Habakkuk 3 marching with Deber, pestilence, as part of the divine warrior's coterie.

That Yahweh's battle against his people is—as is true of his past battles for Israel—an event of war on the human plane is indicated in v 25 with its reference to the sword's destruction. Verses 26 and 27 then give a rather remarkable first person divine statement manifesting the interaction of judgment and mercy and of divine action and human action. Yahweh's inclination toward a judgment of total destruction is modified. He does not follow his bent "to make the remembrance of them cease from among men." But in this case the merciful holding back is for a quite particular reason. Yahweh fears that exile and total destruction at the hand of a human foe will lead the enemy in pride to assume that its might has accomplished this rather than Yahweh's power and will. The divine concern at this point does not imply that other nations are not involved (v 21b announced that they would be). But it guards vigorously the claim that the nations are only instruments (*bᵉgôy*—v 21) and that the agent bringing about or accomplishing judgment through such a nation is Yahweh. All the first person verbs of vv 21–27 confirm the agency of Yahweh. There could be confusion about whether or not Yahweh is bringing this about, so the Lord acts in a way to avoid that confusion. While there is a dimension of correlation between sin and judgment expressed in the detailed correspondence, the poem does not see the judgment as a sort of natural outflow of the sin, even one that Yahweh oversees. Sin and its consequence are intricately interrelated, but Deut 22 insists on the divine decision and the divine agency to bring about vengeance or vindication (*nāqām*) and recompense (v 35). This latter verse (cf. v 41) demonstrates the nuanced way in which judgment involves at one and the same time the working out of the sin and the divine recompense. Yahweh announces his vengeance and his requital, but these will take place "at the time when their foot shall slip."

The Former Prophets

A large number of examples of prophetic announcement of punishment corresponding to the crime occur in the narrative books of the Old Testament. These are virtually all judgment speeches against an individual, i.e. a prophet against a king. Over half the judgment speeches in Samuel and Kings manifest this characteristic, most of them coming from prophets of the tenth to eighth centuries. While some of the instances discussed below may reflect a narrative or redactional creation of the correspondence of sin and judgment, the evidence suggests a somewhat greater tendency toward formulation of the correlation in earlier prophetic oracles than later.

2 Samuel 12

We may take as an example one of the earliest prophetic judgment speeches against an individual, Nathan's oracle to David following the Bathsheba-Uriah incident (2 Sam 12:7–15). In its entirety—both in its general judgment and in particulars—sin and judgment coincide.

The oracle is an outgrowth of the narrative of royal injustice in 2 Sam 11. The sin of David is a dual one—adultery and murder. Both sins are accomplished by the prerogatives and possibilities of royal power. Theologically, what David did was interpreted as evil before Yahweh, his God. All of these aspects of the sinfulness are spelled out at length or in short in the narrative of 2 Sam 11. They are then taken up both in the accusation of the judgment speech and in the announcement of judgment. The particular sin of David is declared in 2 Sam 12:9.

> You have struck Uriah the Hittite with the sword, and have taken his wife to be your wife, and have killed him with the sword of the Ammonites.

The sin is twofold according to this description: He has killed Uriah with the sword; and he has taken his wife (this indictment would include David's taking Bathsheba before and after Uriah's death). The *baḥereb* modification is not unimportant. It points to the fact that David accomplished Uriah's murder through the means of war—a statement of fact but also an anticipation of the judgment to come.

The announcement of that judgment follows in vv 10–11, placing upon David a punishment appropriate at both points. The accusation of murder placed its emphasis on the means by which David accomplished this treachery: "with the sword" (9b), "with the sword of the Ammonites" (9a). So in a variation on the more familiar formula Nathan pronounces the divine judgment that the one who kills by the sword will be forced to live by the sword: "Now, therefore (*wᵉʿattāh*), the sword shall never depart from your house . . ." (v 10). David by his sin of using the devices and implements of war has brought upon himself the doom of having to contend with those devices and implements throughout his life and that of his dynasty.

The other aspect of David's sin was that of taking another man's wife for his own (*lāqaḥ* + *ʾiššāh*). Like the point about the sword this indictment is also made twice (vv 9b and 10b). The punishment pronounced for such a sin is exceedingly appropriate: The one who takes a wife (*lāqaḥ* + *ʾiššāh*—vv 9 and 10) will have his wives taken and given to another (*lāqaḥ* + *nāšîm*—v 11).

In both aspects the punishment is a classic example of the talion notion. In the second element it is fairly precise: *lāqaḥ ʾiššāh . . . lāqaḥ nāšîm*. The first element of judgment is not precise but represents a talionic variation not unlike other instances of the way the prophets play on this correspondence motif, using the instrument or means of sin and of judgment as the focus.

We have noted also that another dimension of David's sin is the fact that it involved an oppressive and unjust use of royal power and privilege. That is indicated both in the narrative of chapter 11 itself and especially in the parable Nathan tells to David in 12:1–6. This aspect also of David's sinfulness is then picked up and underscored in the accusation and announcement of the judgment speech. The divine speech in which the accusation is couched begins with a cataloguing of the ways Yahweh has made David king and the divine gifts of kingship which Yahweh has bestowed on David: anointed king, delivered from Saul, given Saul's house and Saul's wives, given the house of Israel and Judah (vv 7–8). Then in the announcement of the punishment it is made clear that both aspects of the punishment affect not just David as a person but David as king and the monarchy he will establish. Both aspects have to do with David's "house" (vv 10, 11). In the first instance the punishment is that David and his successors as kings will have to endure wars in and against their kingdom forever. The abuse of kingship means punishment against the king. In the second instance the punishment again affects the king as king. Evil will come from his own house, i.e. his own line. And it is of a particular kind—public intercourse with the king's wives. While on the one hand that fits the talionic character of the punishment, something further is obviously intended. For the public taking of the king's wives is clearly a challenge to David's kingship and must be understood as an effort to take it away. That is the real point of its being done publicly over against David's private actions. Not only, therefore, are the particular sins met with an appropriate punishment, but David's misuse of his royal office means that that office will be under continual threat and danger. The punishment corresponds fairly closely to the kind of curse one finds in the vassal treaties of Esarhaddon:

> May Venus, the brightest among the stars, let your wives lie in the embrace of your enemy before your very eyes, may your sons not have authority over your house, may a foreign enemy divide your possessions.[1]

The poetic justice of David's deed works itself out, or, more accurately, is worked out by Yahweh, in one further respect. Not infrequently the correlation of sin and punishment may center upon the purpose or result of the sin. That is the case here. The account of Uriah's death in 2 Sam 11 reports that after the time of mourning was over, David brought Bathsheba to his house as his wife, and she bore him a son. Then the final word of judgment and the first act of judgment deal with this immediate result of David's double sin. The child dies.

Finally, the theological character of David's sin as wickedness before Yahweh is taken up out of the story and made a focus of the judgment speech in a way that is typical in the Deuteronomistic History and present also in the prophets. The concluding sentence of the story states: "The thing which David did was evil (*yēra'*) in the eyes of Yahweh" (11:27b). The accusation part of the judgment speech picks up this theological statement when the prophet says:

> Why have you despised the word of Yahweh to do what is evil (*hāra'*) in his eyes?

Then in the announcement of judgment a punishment is announced appropriate to one who has done *ra'* in the eyes of Yahweh. Yahweh will do *ra'* to him:

> Behold I will raise up evil (*rā'āh*) against you from your own house . . .

This general theological statement, which is spelled out in both cases as to the particulars of David's *ra'* and of Yahweh's *rā'(āh)*, is a kind of paradigm of the correspondence motif in its most general expression. *Ra'* leads to *ra'*. The *ra'* (evil) of the sin leads to the *ra'* (punishment) of the judgment. A model is thus produced to express the correspondence device *in nuce*: *ra'* (human)—*ra'* (divine). This general model undergirds the form of the correspondence in several other examples and in some sense may be presumed to be the theological basis of the correspondence between sin and judgment in general.

While the pronouncements of judgment throughout this passage have an appropriateness for both the crimes and the criminal, they are not merely empty words. The story of David and the Davidic dynasty bears testimony

[1] *ANET Supplement*, 538. Note that both the treaty and the judgment speech announce that the king's wives will lie in the embrace of another "before your very eyes."

to the way this punishment which fit the sin and the sinner worked itself out in history. Indeed the sword never departed David's house (cf. 2 Sam 21:15–22 for David's own reign). Even more significant, the announcement that David's wives would be given to another, who would be with them in the sun and before Israel, reached its fulfillment, not in a literal way but in continuity with the announcement when Absalom set up a tent on the roof and went in to his father's concubines in the sight of all Israel. Thus the *ra'* of David was met by the *ra'* of Yahweh.

1 Samuel 2:27–36

The judgment declared by the man of God against Eli and his house offers us another example of the correspondence motif in the books of Samuel. While some of the conclusions of this narrative may be Deuteronomistic and a later addition, as a whole the narrative is an early account of the Elide sin and punishment that is worked out in 1 Sam 4ff.[2] The heart of the correspondence is the judgment that because the Elides used their position to grow rich and fat, they will end up cut off both from their position and from their prosperity. The correspondence is expressed in general theological terms not unlike 1 Sam 15:23b (see below) and in a somewhat talionic mode in v 30b;

> Far be it from me: for those who honor me (*m^{e}kabbeday*) I will honor (*'^{a}kabbēd*), and those who despise me (*bōzay*) shall be lightly esteemed (*yēqāllû*).

In the first sentence the same verb expresses human action and divine response; in the second sentence the verbs change but they still express the correspondence. The punishment is like the sin: despising God leads to being despised by God. Furthermore in 3:13 the reason for Yahweh's punishment of Eli and his house is given again as follows:

> *ba'^{a}wôn '^{a}šer - yāda' kî - m^{e}qal^{e}lîm '^{e}lōhîm*[3] *bānāw*
> for the iniquity which he knew, because his sons were slighting God.

Here the sin is expressed with exactly the same words used to express Yahweh's punishment in 2:30b.[4]

The correspondence is also expressed with the same precise language in vv 29 and 32. Verse 20 reads

> *lāmmāh tib'^{a}ṭu b^{e}zibḥî ûb^{e}minḥātî '^{a}šer ṣiwwîtî mā'ôn.*
> Why do you look at my sacrifices and my offerings which I commanded . . . ?

[2] See the discussion in P. D. Miller and J. J. M. Roberts, *The Hand of the Lord: A Reassessment of the "Ark Narrative" of I Samuel* (Baltimore: The Johns Hopkins University Press, 1977) 27–31.

[3] Reading *'^{e}lōhîm* of LXX for MT's *lāhem*.

[4] Cf. M. Tsevat, "Studies in the Book of Samuel," *HUCA* 32 (1961) 203.

The meaning of *mā'ôn* is uncertain. It seems to have to do with how Eli looks at the sacrifices—covetously, greedily, etc. Settling the meaning, however, of *mā'ôn* is not necessary for the purposes of this discussion.[5] The point is that a similar idiom is used in the announcement of punishment in v 32: *w^e^hibbaṭṭā ṣar mā'ôn*, "Then in distress you will look (*mā'ôn*?) on all that he has caused Israel to prosper." The punishment of the Elides will be appropriate to their sin. It is to have the same attitudes and desires but be unable to fill them.

1 Samuel 15:10–31

A still earlier prophetic judgment that both grows out of a narrative and helps shape it is Samuel's denunciation of Saul for sparing Agag and Amalekite booty after Yahweh had commanded the *ḥērem*. The form of this is not as precisely a judgment speech as other passages identified here, but the intention is the same. Samuel characterizes the sin of Saul as disobedience, rebellion, and stubbornness. Then he climaxes this indictment by summarizing it and announcing a punishment that corresponds exactly to the sin.

> Because you have rejected (*mā'astā*) the
> word of the Lord,
> he has rejected you (*wayyim'ās^e^kā*)
> from being king. (15:23b)

The correspondence pattern here provides the structure of the whole narrative and the turning point in the history of Saul. The verses prior to v 23 describe the sin of Saul which is then succinctly defined in v 23ba. In the final colon of this verse the judgment is given, and the rest of the chapter and following chapters describe the working out of the judgment under the rubric of the thematic word *mā'as*. Verse 26 repeats the correlation of sin and punishment given in verse 23b. Then in chapter 16 reference is made twice to Yahweh's "rejection" of Saul (vv 1 and 7).

1 Samuel 15:33

The story of Saul's encounter with Agag and the Amalekites contains another important example of the correlation of crime and punishment in the words of Samuel to Agag as he kills him:

> As (*ka'^a^šer*) your sword has made women
> (*nāšîm*) childless (*šikk^e^lāh*),

[5] In light of the textual evidence one probably should reconstruct the text here as follows:
lmh tbyṭ bzbḥy
wbmnḥty m'wyn
Why do you gaze upon my sacrifice,
and upon my offering cast a greedy eye.
See Miller and Roberts, *The Hand of the Lord* . . . , 30 and 98, n. 14.

so (*kēn*) shall your mother be childless
(*tiškal*) among women (*minnāšîm*).

The correlation is explicitly set up by the comparison formula *ka'ašer* . . . *kēn*. It is his crime and his punishment, though the latter happens in a somewhat different fashion than is usually the case. The verb as a description of his punishment refers not to Agag but to his mother. The result, however, is an even sharper correlation. His sin is making women childless; his punishment is the same—a woman, his mother, is made childless. The punishment is not unexpected nor arbitrary. Agag was a military leader frequently at war and could have expected a violent death as a result of his encounters with his enemies. In this particular instance he thought he was safe, only to suffer the common fate of vanquished enemies. Samuel's words create a poetic justice and thus characterize Agag's death as a retributive justice. The death of Agag is not explicitly announced as Yahweh's judgment, but the original command (15:2–3), the correlation of crime and punishment, and the indication that Samuel killed Agag "before Yahweh" (15:33) suggest that Agag's death is to be understood as divine judgment.

1 Kings 21:17–24

When we move to the ninth century we encounter an excellent example of the correspondence of sin and punishment in Elijah's pronouncement of judgment against Ahab after the Naboth incident (1 Kgs 21:17–24). The character of this passage as a judgment speech has been well analyzed by Westermann, though he focuses only on vv 18–19, presumably because of the character of vv 20–24 as a Deuteronomistic addition to the Elijah judgment speech.[6] Both parts of this passage will occupy our attention.

Like the Samuel passages, these verses grow out of a narrative. Even as did David, Ahab has used the powers and influence of the monarchy to carry out an act of injustice. David used the military machinery; Ahab uses the judicial machinery. Elijah is sent to confront Ahab in the act of taking Naboth's vineyard. The judgment speech proper is given in v 19:

	Thus says the Lord:
Accusation/Indictment	Have you killed, and also taken possession?
	Thus says the Lord:
Announcement of Punishment	In the place where dogs licked up the blood of Naboth shall dogs lick your own blood.

The crime is murder and confiscation as the indictment indicates. The punishment corresponding to Ahab's killing Naboth is that he will be killed. That is expressed in the announcement of punishment in vivid language to

[6] C. Westermann, *Basic Forms of Prophetic Speech*, 130ff.

show the precise correlation: Ahab's life for Naboth's life. The reference to the dogs licking up the blood is a particularly powerful mode of expression, but such language is clearly used for more than just its potency.

The second part of the indictment refers to Ahab's act of confiscation. The taking of the vineyard is the point of the judicial murder. By formulating the announcement of punishment as is done here: "In the place where the dogs lick the blood . . ." emphasis is given not just to Ahab's death but to "*the place.*" We are not told in 1 Kings 21 where Naboth was stoned, except that it was outside the city (v 13). One may infer that the announcement of punishment has in mind the vineyard of Naboth the Jezreelite as the place where the dogs will lick Ahab's blood. That inference is underscored by v 23 which carries the correspondence motif over to Jezebel: "The dogs shall eat Jezebel within the bounds of Jezreel" (cf. 2 Kgs 9:36–37). That this is the proper understanding of *bimqôm* in v 19 is made clear by the account of the death of Joram, Ahab's son and the variant form of Elijah's oracle quoted by Jehu over the body of Joram (2 Kgs 9:21–26). The narrative first reports that Joram, king of Israel, and Ahaziah, king of Judah, went out in their chariots to meet Jehu and came upon him (*wayyimṣā'uhû*) at the property (*bᵉḥelqat*) of Naboth the Jezreelite. At that spot Jehu kills the son of Ahab and tells his aide to throw Joram's body on the plot of ground (*bᵉḥelqat śᵉdê*) belonging to Naboth the Jezreelite. Then he quotes the earlier divine word of judgment against Ahab:

> As sure as I saw yesterday the blood of Naboth and the blood of his sons—oracle of Yahweh—I will requite (*šillamtî*) you on this plot of ground. Now, therefore, take him up and throw him on the plot of ground in accordance with the word of the Lord (2 Kgs 9:26).

The narrator at every point wants to underscore the correlation of sin and punishment, the poetic—or better, prophetic justice which Yahweh enacts. Not only is the place of the crime the place of punishment, but the narrative now includes a correlation of the death of Naboth and *his sons* with the death of Ahab's son, Joram.

So Joram's body was thrown onto Naboth's plot and Jezebel's corpse eaten by the dogs in the territory of Jezreel. The locus and reason for the sin of Ahab and Jezebel became also the locus of their punishment. Talionic notions and poetic justice combine in the prophetic proclamation of judgment. And while the working out of this poetic justice was not precisely in accord with the announcement, it was—like the word to Eli—similar enough to lead one to the judgment that the correspondence motif not only carries the prophetic word with special force, but points to a clear continuity between the prophetic pattern—according to the sin, so the punishment—and the realities of history as experienced by individuals and communities.

The Deuteronomistic elaboration in vv 20–24 expresses the correspondence again but in general fashion and in a manner already familiar from

2 Sam 12 and elsewhere. In v 20 Elijah gives the indictment against Ahab: You have sold yourself to do evil (*hāra'*) in the eyes of Yahweh (cf. 2 Sam 11:27 and 12:9). The punishment for one who does *ra'* before Yahweh is that Yahweh will do *ra'* to him: Behold, I am bringing you a judgment (*rā'āh*) (v 21). The rest of vv 21–24 then proceed to spell out that *rā'āh* more or less in typically Deuteronomistic language. Thus once again the theological paradigm appears: human *ra'* = sin—divine *ra'* = judgment.

One should note also at this point what seems to be typical of these judgment speeches against individuals, that the correspondence is substantive and explicit. It is not a correspondence of language, i.e., wordplay, simile, or metaphor. While the correspondence is precise, it tends to be literal in terms of the description of both sin and judgment.

1 Kings 14:7–16

The Deuteronomistic elaboration of Elijah's judgment speech in 1 Kgs 21 is an echo of Ahijah's judgment speech against Jeroboam (1 Kgs 14:7–16). While not all of Ahijah's speech is from the hand of Dtr, the correspondence motif as we find it here undoubtedly is. It is again the familiar paradigm: *ra'* brings *ra'*. The indictment declares: You have done more evil (*wattāra'*) than all who were before you (v 9). The consequent punishment, therefore, is: Behold I will bring evil (*rā'āh*) to the house of Jeroboam (v 10). The example in this regard needs no further comment. The details of the judgment speech are so layered over with Deuteronomistic expressions that it is difficult to capture the original formulation. In any event the correspondence pattern is not evident in the details.

2 Kings 21:10–15

The theological paradigm, *ra'* will be punished with *ra'*, appears again in much the same formulation in the Deuteronomistic judgment against Manasseh. There too Manasseh is said to have done more *evil* than those who were before him, specifically the Amorites. And again the announcement of judgment is made: Behold I will bring *evil* against Jerusalem and Judah.[7]

Then in v 13 two images are used that are not particularly Deuteronomistic. Yahweh declares:

> and I will stretch over Jerusalem the measuring line of Samaria, and the plummet of the house of Ahab; and I will wipe Jerusalem as one wipes a dish, wiping it and turning it upside down.

[7] In addition to its use in Dtr the paradigm human *ra'* leads to divine *rā'(āh)* appears—not surprisingly—several times in Jeremiah: 11:17, 18:7ff., 11; and 26:3. These do not require separate treatment. They are not formal judgment speeches, but represent developments of the *ra'*→*ra'* schema similar to Dtr's formulations.

The imagery of Yahweh measuring his people with line and plumb is not a common one but does appear two or three other times in the Old Testament and is a rather important one for understanding the phenomenon of judgment.

The texts that use this imagery are 2 Kgs 21:13, Isa 28:17; 34:11; and Amos 7:7–9.[8] The *miškōlet* of 2 Kgs 21:13 and Isa 28:17 may be an instrument for measuring horizontal straightness, or vertical straightness, but it is in any event the builder's tool as are the line (*qaw*) and stone (*'eben*). The function of the measuring line and plummet is clear. They are implements to determine if the building is true, the walls straight, and the foundations level. If the walls are not true and the foundations properly laid, the building will not stand. Cracks will appear; walls will eventually give way or fall. The imagery indicates sharply the purposiveness of divine judgment. Negatively, that is seen especially in 2 Kgs 21:13; Isa 34:11, and Amos 7:7–9. Yahweh's measuring of the nation or of Jerusalem is a way of showing that it is not "true." It is off and out of line and thus no longer able to fulfill its proper function. For Yahweh to make this "building" work, he will have to tear it down and start all over. So the divine judgment is announced. 2 Kgs 21:13 and Isa 28:17 indicate how the structure is being measured, negatively by the line of Samaria and the house of Ahab (2 Kgs 21:13) and positively by justice and righteousness (Isa 28:17).

The wiping metaphor is even more unusual. It appears only here in 2 Kgs 21:13 as a figure for judgment. The image seems to function in much the same way as the plumbline, conveying a utilitarian idea. While destruction is clearly indicated—Jerusalem wiped—it is for a purpose. The act is functional and has a larger aim in mind than simply eliminating the food in the dish. It is in order to render the dish, which has a use or function, usable again. Once it is wiped clean Yahweh may use it according to this purpose, may fill it anew. The food that is presently in it is spoiled and rotten. Jerusalem is the dish Yahweh will clean and use again. The image fits perfectly with the historical fate of Jerusalem—wiped clean, turned on its face to be kept till Yahweh is ready to use it again.

2 Kings 17:15 and 20

The long Deuteronomistic sermon on the downfall of the northern kingdom contains an example of the correspondence pattern in these two verses:

15 They rejected (*wayyim'ᵃsû*) his statutes
and his covenant . . .

[8] In an unpublished paper read before the Society of Biblical Literature, Dean McBride has challenged the view that *'nk* in Amos 7:7–9 has to do with a plumb line or that the vision depicts Yahweh measuring his people. If his view should prove correct, this text would be removed from the list. The imagery, however, clearly exists in the other passages mentioned here.

> 20 And Yahweh rejected (*wayyim'as*) all the descendants of Israel.

In this particular case, however, the correspondence is not a dominant element in the passage. The denunciation of Israel's sins is extensive and expressed in many ways. Verse 15 itself characterizes their sin in yet another fashion. In like manner the announcement of judgment (vv 18ff.) describes Yahweh's judgment in various ways, one of which is *wayyim'as bᵉkol zera' yiśrā'ēl*. The corresponding elements are far enough apart, and imbedded in the midst of other verbs of sin and judgment, that one's attention is not caught by the correlation of the two as in the other examples discussed here.

1 Kings 13:1–2

Two other passages in 1 Kgs command our attention, one briefly and the other somewhat more extensively. In the strange story of the man of God at Bethel in 1 Kgs 13 there is a brief judgment speech uttered by the prophet against the altar at Bethel:

> O altar, altar, thus says the Lord: Behold, a son shall be born to the house of David, Josiah by name; and he shall sacrifice upon you the priests of the high places who burn incense upon you, and men's bones shall be burned upon you (v 2).

The correspondence in this case is fairly obvious. The judgment speech gives only the sentence and lacks the indictment. But the indictment is clearly understood from the concluding verses of chapter 12, which refer to the priests of the high places and the burning of incense upon the altar. The Deuteronomist, therefore, supplies the indictment that the altar is non-Yahwistic and the practices belonging to it idolatrous and a sin against Yahweh. The punishment that is appropriate for the pagan altar is that those who sin against Yahweh by officiating at this altar—the priests of the high places—will themselves become a sacrifice on the altar. And the altar which was the occasion of sin against Yahweh by burning incense upon it will become desecrated by the burning of human bones upon it. One notes further that the correspondence between sin and punishment is accentuated by the fact that the words of judgment are not in this instance directed to Jeroboam or the people but to the altar. Their appropriateness is directly related to the fact that the altar itself is the object of judgment. The correspondence motif would not be as sharp if these words had been directed to Jeroboam. In accordance with Dtr's schema of prophecy and fulfillment in the Books of Kings the report of the fulfillment of this prophecy precisely according to the terms stated in 1 Kgs 13:2 is given in 2 Kgs 23:20.

1 Kings 20:42

The next text to be mentioned is quite brief but important for understanding the correspondence pattern in the prophetic judgment speeches. It is the story in 1 Kgs 20 of the encounter between the unnamed prophet and the king of Israel, Ahab, who had come to terms with the captured Ben-hadad rather than putting him to the ban. The prophet says to the king:

> Thus says Yahweh, "Because you have let go out of (your) hand the man of my *ḥērem*, therefore your life shall be in the place of his life and your people in the place of his people."

The passage demonstrates the tenacity of the traditions of holy war in the north, but this is not our immediate concern. The sin of the king is the failure to destroy Ben-hadad as *ḥērem* to Yahweh. Appropriate to the crime is the punishment—Ahab's life for Ben-hadad. The judgment fits the deed. Since Ahab let go of Ben-hadad, then Ahab shall take his place. Failure to enact the *ḥērem* means the *ḥērem* will be enacted against him. The correspondence is explicit and concrete.

What particularly strikes one's attention, however, is the formulation of the correspondence: *nepeš taḥat nepeš*. For that is precisely the form of the *lex talionis* (Exod 21:23 and Lev 24:18; Deut 20:19 uses *bᵉ*- instead of *taḥat*). In other words, the correspondence in this case is explicitly a case of talion, yet it is at the same time clearly the use of the correspondence pattern, a fact that would be evident even if the talion formula were absent and the announcement of judgment simply foretold the death of Ahab. The talion character of the judgment speech is so clear that the prophet actually uses the formula itself. It is something of a reverse use in that the formula usually means a life taken will be punished by a life. Here it is a life kept will be punished by a life taken. But the principle is fundamentally the same, and the application of the formula implies both substitution or compensation and punishment.

The legal-judicial character of this example of the correspondence motif is indicated further by the conversation that preceded the judgment speech. In the encounter between the king and the disguised prophet we have what amounts to an informal court case. The prophet brings a case to the king for judgment and the king renders a *mišpāṭ* or says the prophet has in effect given it himself (v 40). The hypothetical case involved a soldier supposedly placing a prisoner in the prophet's hands with the instructions:

> Keep this man; if by any means he be missing your life shall be for his life (*napšᵉkā taḥat napšô*) or else you shall pay a talent of silver (*kikkar kesep tišqōl*) (v 39).

Here again is the talion formula which is cited in the judgment speech and expanded to include the people. But in this case the legal character of what is being said is accentuated by the casuistic form and the addition of a proviso for monetary compensation rather than substitution. The expression *šāqal kesep* also appears in the Book of the Covenant (Exod 22:16).

In this passage, therefore, we have an excellent example of the correspondence device or pattern and one that is formulated in legal terminology and set in the context of an informal judicial setting. Now while the individuality of all the examples of correspondence, including this one, must be maintained and while the sin or crime that is judged in this case is particularly relevant to the idea of substitution contained in the *lex talionis*, this last example may provide an important clue to one of the settings of the correspondence motif.

Joshua 7:25

Two passages in the narratives of the Former Prophets do not reflect prophetic judgment words but belong under consideration here because of their very clear use of the correspondence pattern. One of them, the story of Achan's sin and execution in Josh 7, is virtually built out of this pattern. In verse 25 after Achan has confessed his sin Joshua says:

> *meh ʿākartānû yaʿkorkā yhwh bayyôm hazzeh*
> Why did you bring trouble on us? Yahweh brings trouble on you today.

The first sentence is the indictment of Achan for his sin. The second sentence announces his punishment. Indeed what is described here is in skeletal form a judicial process that centers upon this correspondence between sin and judgment and the root *ʿkr*. The instruction about the *ḥērem* and how it is to be carried out against Jericho is given in 6:17ff. It includes the stipulation to keep from taking anything under the ban "lest you . . . put the camp under the ban and *bring trouble* (*waʿakartem*) on it." The command of Joshua is not the promulgation of a legal statute, but it is a requirement of the holy war that is to follow, and he gives it to the people as a binding statute in the ensuing conflict: Don't take of the *ḥērem* lest you place the camp under the ban and bring trouble on it.[9] Then Joshua and *all Israel* take Achan, his family, and his possessions up to the Plain[10] of Achor. In effect Joshua and the people move to act as a cultic-judicial assembly to render *mišpāṭ*. The name of the place where justice and judgment are to be carried out is, of course, quite intentional in the narrative and underscores the issue and the correspondence of sin and judgment. It is *ʿēmeq ʿākôr*, "the plain of *trouble*." In this Plain of Trouble Joshua first indicts Achan for his sin: *ʿākartānû*—You have brought trouble. Then he announces in the assembly the verdict or judgment: *yaʿkorkā yhwh*—Yahweh will bring trouble on you. The assembly proceeds, therefore, to carry out the punishment. In the same Plain of Trouble Achan and all that belongs to him are stoned and burned by all the people (cf. Lev 24:14b and 16b).

[9] See W. Preiser, "Vergeltung und Sühne im altisraelitischen Strafrecht," *Um das Prinzip der Vergeltung*, 253, who speaks of Achan's sin as a transgression of a requirement generally based in the covenant order of Yahweh that in this case is concretized by command of the military leader, Joshua.

[10] So M. Noth, *Das Buch Josua*² (HAT; Tübingen: J. C. B. Mohr, 1953) 21.

The narrative thus recounts an occasion of judicial administration in which in talionic fashion a sharp correlation is made between sin and punishment. It is most transparent in the judgment speech from the lips of Joshua: *'ākar—'ākar*. But the correspondence in the judgment speech which is so familiar from the prophetic oracles is carried much further and becomes in effect a theme if not *the* theme of the narrative. It is elaborated in such a way that to a large extent the narrative is developed around the point of correspondence: *'ākar* = trouble. This may be seen at several points, at least some of which represent stages in the growth of the narrative wherein this theme is increasingly heightened:

(a) the correspondence of sin and judgment around the verb *'ākar* in 7:25.
(b) the anticipation of this correspondence in 6:18 in the command not to *'ākar* the camp.
(c) the setting of the judgment speech and the execution at *'ēmeq 'ākôr*.
(d) the aetiological note in 7:26 indicating that the name of that place is called *'ēmeq 'ākôr 'ad hayyôm hazzeh*.
(e) the wordplay between the name of the one who sins and is punished (*'ākān*), the nature of his sin and of his punishment (*'ākar*), and the place of judgment (*'ākôr*), i.e., the repetition of the *'āk*-element.
(f) the genealogy in 1 Chronicles 2:7 which gives the name of *'Ākān* as *'Ākār* and characterizes him as *'ākār 'ôkēr yiśrā'ēl*.
(g) the Septuagint's leveling through of the name as *achar* wherever it occurs in the chapter.

It may be assumed that these developments occurred roughly in the order given above though not all of them need to have been discrete or separate stages (for example, a and b may belong together; so also c and d).

While the narrative is not associated with prophecy, it is an important example in the context of this study for two reasons. Like the story of David and Bathsheba and its aftermath as well as to a lesser extent other narratives in the historical books (e.g. 1 Kgs 21) the correspondence of sin and judgment in Josh 7:25 is elaborated and worked out in an extended way within a narrative so that it becomes thematic and the story is made quite dependent upon an explicit correlation. Further, the narrative provides another case in which the correspondence of sin and punishment is set within a judicial process, suggesting at least in part the setting in life in which this correlation functioned, the movement from statute to crime to judicial process culminating in punishment.

The reader hears (literally, when one takes into account the repeated words and the wordplay) clearly the central word of the passage (*'ākar*) and is enabled to integrate the whole story around this note. Yahweh's justice corresponds to the crime. The story affirms the interrelation of judgment speech announcing *God's* action in the punishment (Yahweh will bring trouble on you) and the deed of judgment which is carried out by *human* agents (all Israel stoned him with stones).

Judges 1:7

The account in Judg 1 of territories acquired by the Israelites from the Canaanites and those still remaining in Canaanite hands contains a brief report of an incident in which a correspondence is noted between the punishment carried out by the Israelites against the captured king Adoni-bezeq and similar actions done by him to previous kings. The Israelites cut off the thumbs and big toes of Adoni-bezeq. Whereupon he declares: "Seventy kings with their thumbs and their great toes cut off used to pick up scraps under my table; as I have done, so God has requited me (*ka'^{a}šer 'āśîtî kēn šillam-lî '^{e}lōhîm*)" (1:7). As Adoni-bezeq's remark indicates, this particular kind of punishment was his way of indicating defeat and subjection of an enemy king. In this case it is not so much that Adoni-bezeq has sinned and an appropriate punishment is carried out against him as it is that the fate which other defeated kings received at his hands becomes now his own fate as a defeated king.[11]

The king's concluding statement, "As I have done, so God has requited me," is similar to the talionic formulation in Lev 24:19–20; "As he has done, so shall it be done to him." Two differences may be noted. One is the fact that God is the one who repays Adoni-bezeq as he has done in the past. The action is seen by the one who suffers it as the action of God although the narrative indicates clearly that the Israelites carried out the deed. The correspondence is perceived as a part of divine justice, not simply human vengeance. The formulation in Judg 1:7 contrasts with Lev 24:19–20 also in that the verb *šillēm* is used to characterize Yahweh's action. The difference is not as great as might seem at first glance. In Jer 50:29 a formulation similar to that in Judg 1:7 appears parallel to one like Lev 24:19–20.

> *šall^{e}mû lāh k^{e}po'^{o}lāh*
> *k^{e}kōl '^{a}šer 'āś^{e}tāh '^{a}śû lāh*
> Requite her according to her deed;
> according to all that she has done,
> do to her.

While the incident itself may have the character of *Tun-Ergehen* in that one can see in the earlier deeds of Adoni-bezeq the inevitable moment when he will be forced into subjection as he forced other kings, that idea is not inherent in *šillēm*. The verb indicates rather that God has freely decided to pay back Adoni-bezeq for his deeds to others.[12]

The passage demonstrates, therefore, with regard to both the question of agency and the question of retribution the kind of double-sided character

[11] On the question whether Adoni-bezeq's mutilating habit was peculiar to him or a general custom in regard to captured kings, see commentaries and B. S. Jackson, "The Problem of Exodus 21:22–25 (*ius talionis*)," *Essays in Jewish and Comparative Legal History* (Leiden: E. J. Brill, 1975) 83.

[12] Cf. J. Scharbert, "ŠLM im Alten Testament," *Um das Prinzip der Vergeltung*, 316–17.

that has been noted in previous passages. The narrative recounts a military endeavor between Judah and Simeon and the Canaanites and Perizzites that culminates in the capture of Adoni-bezeq and his maiming by the Israelites. But in and through that human activity Adoni-bezeq experiences the judgment of God. He does not say: ". . . so it has been done to me." He says, ". . . so *God* has requited me." And the peculiar punishment Adoni-bezeq receives, in the light of his recollection of his own maiming of captured kings, seems to belong to the *schicksalwirkender Tatsphäre* (Koch's term), while in the light of his interpretation of his punishment as God's requital, the correspondence points to the punishment as divine retribution effected not by the fate-decreeing earlier deeds (even if one sees Yahweh as calling that fate forth) but by the free and independent decision of Yahweh to punish Adoni-bezeq.

CHAPTER II

The Source and Setting of the Correspondence Pattern

The movement from description of how the rhetoric and meaning of correspondence are expressed in individual passages to the question of its source and setting is a large and difficult step. Indeed any steps in this direction must have a tentativeness to them. But there are questions that need to be raised however tentative our answers may be. To what setting(s) or context(s) does the correspondence pattern belong? Can the modes of correlation discussed here be seen as deriving from ways of speaking or literary formulation that belong to other areas of life? If so, how does that color the prophetic word?

In the search for setting of a literary mode or speech style, two things need to be said at the beginning. First of all, the prophetic correlation of sin and judgment may not have a precise setting to which it can be traced. We are not dealing here, in my judgment, with a *Gattung* or genre for which one should expect a setting in life—though the correlation of sin and judgment seems in the prophets to be related to or associated with certain genres that may have some significance for the question of setting of the pattern itself (see below). Indeed it should be said at the beginning that the correspondence pattern as a dimension of style involving figures of speech, paranomasia, and repetition and conveying irony and poetic justice belongs to universal patterns of speech and stylistic modes so that they cannot always be neatly connected to some source outside the canons of literary and artistic achievement. The correspondence device in a sense belongs to the storeroom of materials available to the prophet, poet, or speaker, whoever he or she might be.

Having said that much, however, and without diminishing the point, one may continue the analogy by noting that such materials do come from somewhere and some of them may have a special character to them that leads the poet or prophet to choose them. The many instances of poetic justice which appear in proverbial and other wisdom literature reflect a notion of order in the world that surely has something to do with the formation of such sayings. So in prophetic literature the correspondence of sin and judgment may reflect settings and contexts that are important to the prophetic message or have connotations beyond their obvious rhetorical potential. That likelihood is increased by the recognition of three things in the prophetic usage:

(a) the correlation of sin and punishment as described in these pages is primarily associated with a particular type of speech;
(b) in some narrative instances of correspondence a setting beyond prophetic proclamation is suggested;
(c) in several instances of correspondence in both oracles and narratives certain words, formulas, and sub-types point to association with particular settings or traditions.

The second preliminary assertion, which grows out of the above and is a sort of corollary of the conclusion that examples of correspondence may not have to arise from any particular setting, is the possibility if not the likelihood of multiple settings, sources, or contexts for this pattern of speech. The evidence from the sources suggests at least three possibilities. We shall take them up one by one.

I. One possible source for the correspondence of sin and judgment is what has already been suggested, i.e. the general and fairly universal patterns of speech and style wherein poetic justice is a common literary device. One can find examples in myths, fairy stories, fables, legends, novels, and other genres from various locales. It should be expected that the prophetic correlation of sin and judgment has its roots partially in the general literary usage of poetic justice and irony. While this setting needs no elaboration, it is surely a part of the background of prophetic usage.

II. In his study of Hos 4:4–6 Lohfink has pointed to similarities between the correspondence of sin and judgment by repetition of the same verbs in both West-Semitic curse formulations as well as the "parity style" of international diplomatic communication, particularly, though not only, in treaties and covenant.[1] Lohfink treats these as separate types and settings for the correspondence of verbs which indeed they are. But there are sufficient relationships between the categories to connect them and see them as part of the curse type generally as protection for "documents" and as sanction for and insurer of obedience to treaty or covenant.

Several examples of curse formulas for protection of various sorts of inscriptions can be cited. The Kilamuwa inscription concludes:

> Whoever smashes (*yšḥt*) this inscription,
> may Ba'l Samad of Gabbar smash (*yšḥt*) his head and may Ba'l-Hamman of Bmh and Rakabel the lord of the house smash (*wyšḥt*) his head. (1.15f.)[2]

In a similar fashion the Azitawadda inscription from Karatepe concludes with a lengthy curse as a protection of the inscription and the name and fame of Azitawadda:

> If there be a king among kings and a prince among princes or a man who is (just) called a man who shall wipe out (*ymḥ*) the name of Azitawadda from this gate and

[1] Lohfink, "Zu Text und Form . . . ," *Biblica* 42 (1961) 314ff.

[2] See H. Donner and W. Röllig, *Kanaanäische und Aramäische Inschriften* (Wiesbaden: O. Harrassowitz, 1964) No. 24.

> put down his own name, even if he has good intentions toward this city but removes the gate which was made by Azitawadda and makes for the (new) gate a (new) "frame" and puts his name upon it, whether he removes this gate with good intentions or out of hatred and evil, let Ba'lshamen and El-the-Creator-of-the-Earth and the Eternal-Sun and the whole Group of the children (*wmḥ*) of the Gods (El) wipe out (*wmḥ*) that ruler and that king and that man who is (just) called a man! However, the name of Azitawadda shall endure forever like the name of sun and moon![3]

In both these cases the gods are invoked to punish the one destroying the inscription and thus the name, memory, and position of the subject by doing to him as he has done to the inscription (*šḥt, mḥh*). One can find similar curses in other locales. For example, in the Egyptian Biographical Inscriptions the address to the grave visitor is often accompanied by a curse if the visitor does not honor the grave site and a promise to the one who does: "All that you should do towards my grave will also be done toward your grave."[4] The Nerab I stele, referred to in the discussion of Isa 1:19–20, also has a "protection clause" formulated as blessing rather than curse and repeating the verb:

> But if you guard (*nṣr*) this image and grave,
> In the future may yours be guarded (*nṣr*) (11.11–14)

We note further that the same sort of protection clause appears in a treaty document, Stele I from Sefire:

> May (he who observes the words of this stela) be guarded by the Gods as to his day and as to his house. But whoever does not observe the words of the inscription on this stela but says: I shall "efface" some of its words, or I shall upset (*'hpk*) the good things and put (*w'šm*) down evil ones, on the day he will do so, that man and his house and all that is in it shall be upset (*yhpkw*) by the God and "he (his house)" be turned upside down (*wyšmw*), and that man shall not "acquire" a name.[5]

The correspondence in this case is somewhat more complex than in the previous examples. Whoever overturns good, will himself be overturned. Literally the text says the one who puts good in the place of evil, i.e. reverses things, will have his lower part put as his upper part. In other words, he will be reversed. The correspondence involves repetition of verbs (*hpk*

[3] *ANET*³, 654–55.

[4] In an unpublished paper read to a section of the 1974 Society of Biblical Literature, Katherine Havice has discussed the correspondence notion in these inscriptions, which frequently involves the repetition of verbs, sometimes in a lengthy series. The correspondence has to do with both positive and negative actions for reward and punishment. "The Concern for the Widow and the Fatherless: The Setting and Function of the Concern in the Egyptian Biographical Form."

[5] See Donner and Röllig, *Kanaanäische und Aramäische Inschriften*, No. 222 C. Note the verb *nṣr* is used here also to carry the correspondence (15, 17, and B. 1. 8). Cf. *ANET*, 660 for the translation given here.

and *šym*) but also correspondence of ideas. Reversal (of good and evil) leads to reversal (of the lower and upper parts of the evil doer and his house).[6]

As Lohfink observes, this curse is not a part of the curses for keeping the treaty, which are listed *in extenso* on this stele. But the curse does in a sense safeguard the treaty and continue to protect it and guard its observance. While the correspondence is specifically in terms of the one who overturns good and puts evil, this is understood as the action of one who "does not observe the words of the inscription." The curse does have to do with protection of the treaty obligations and not merely protection of the written form of it. In this sense it can be related to what Baltzer has called the *Grundsatzerklärung* and what Korosec has identified as the essence of the Hittite vassal treaties, the mutual obligation of protection, which, as Lohfink points out, can be taken over from the middle part of the treaty into the blessings and curses.[7] He cites the treaty of Muwattalis and Alaksandus:

> Wenn du aber diese Worte bewahrst (*paḫḫašti*), so sollen diese tausend Götter . . . dich . . . gutig beschützen (*paḫšantaru*).

Correspondence by repetition in such protection stipulations and curses is not required, but it is there on a number of occasions. The curses of the Kilamuwa, Karatepe, and Nerab (blessing) steles function like the examples above from Sefire and other treaties but in the latter case the blessings and curses have to do with keeping and observing the treaty. The same is the case in the covenant tradition of Israel where the mutual obligation of keeping and protecting the covenant is expressed, for example, in Deut 7:8ff. where curses come when the words are not kept. (Note the repetition of *šāmar* here; cf. Exod 19:5, 20:6, and Deut 28:15).

Lohfink brings into consideration also Joshua 7 with its central use of the correspondence pattern, especially in v 25 (see preceding chapter). The act of Achan is characterized twice as a breach or transgression of covenant (vv 11 and 15) and the correlation of sin and punishment is related to the stipulation of sacral warfare not to take anything under the ban *lest one bring trouble on the camp* (6:18). A sacral judicial process takes place to determine the guilty one and punish him for that breach of covenant. While the instruction of Joshua is not formulated as a curse, the *pen* clause clearly

[6] In this connection compare the curse in Deut 28:43.

> The sojourner who is among you shall mount above you higher and higher; and you shall come down lower and lower.

[7] "Doch selbst in den mittleren Vertragsteil, der die Verpflichtungen des Vasallen beschreibt, tritt der Gedanke der Gegenseitigkeit ein. Die konkreten Einzelverpflichtungen sind nämlich meist einer Art Dachklausel im Paritätestil untergeordnet: der Klausel von der gegenseitigen Schutzpflicht. Und hier begegnen wir wiedrum oft wiederholten Tätigkeitsworten. Der Stilzug konnte dann aus dem mittleren Teil des Vertrags, der die Bedingungen enthielt, in der abschliessenden Segen-und Fluchteil übernommen werden . . . ," Lohfink, "Zu Text und Form . . . ," 318–19.

functions as a sanction against disobedience of the covenant and is itself an example of correspondence of sin and punishment.

> But you keep yourself from the *ḥērem* lest when you have devoted/banned them, you take from the *ḥērem* and put the camp of Israel to *ḥērem* and trouble it.

Equally significant for a possible setting of the correspondence of sin and punishment in the context of covenant curses is the existence of a kind of correspondence that takes place apparently directly in relation to these curses. These do not come into Lohfink's view because the correspondence in this case does not generally happen through the repetition of verbs, which is the type of correspondence to which he confines himself, but in terms of the result of the sin. That is, the punishment is the frustration of the intention or the intended result of the sinful action. Examples of these that we have encountered are Amos 5:7, 10–11; Isa 5:8–10; 28:14–18; 30:1–5; Hos 4:7–10; Mic 2:1–5; 3:9–12. Other examples may involve some frustration of the result, but these at least do so as a direct part of the correspondence.

As we noted in discussion of these passages, several of them have direct connection with the so-called "futility curses" of some of the Near Eastern treaties of the first millennium and the curses of Lev 26 and Deut 28.[8] The two best examples of these are provided by Amos 5:7, 10–11 and Isa 5:8–10. In the former case the announcement of judgment reiterates the sin with more specificity and gives the judgment (v 11):

> Therefore, because you trample upon the poor
> and take from him exactions of wheat,
> you have built houses,
> but you shall not dwell in them;
> you have planted pleasant vineyards,
> but you shall not drink their wine.

With this one may compare Deut 28:30:

> You shall build a house, and you shall not dwell in it; you shall plant a vineyard, and you shall not use the fruit of it.

or 28:39:

> You shall plant vineyards and dress them,
> but you shall neither drink of the wine nor
> gather the grapes; for the worm shall eat them.

Isa 5:8–10 depicts a similar punishment involving houses and fields acquired that remain desolate and yield little fruit. In like manner the announcement concerning the priests in Hos 4:10:

[8] On these curses see D. R. Hillers, *Treaty Curses and the Old Testament Prophets* (Rome: Pontifical Biblical Institute, 1964) 28ff.

> They shall eat and not be satisfied;
> they have played the harlot but will not increase

may be compared with the Sefire curses that sheep will mate but not become pregnant, children and animals suckle but not be satisfied (cf. Mic 6:14, with particular reference to the translation by Mays).[9]

As further association of the correspondence pattern with the covenant curses, two passages should be mentioned which demonstrate correspondence of sin and judgment by means of repetition of verbs and the paradigm *ra'* ⟶ *ra'*. The first is Deut 28:47–48.

> Because you did not serve (*lō' - 'ābadtā*) the Lord your God with joyfulness and goodness of heart by reason of the abundance of everything, therefore you shall serve (*w^e'ābadtā*) your enemies whom the Lord shall send against you . . .

Here is the fundamental stipulation of the covenant (Exod 20:4–6 = Deut 5:8–10). Israel that does not serve Yahweh but serves other gods (Deuteronomy *passim*) will find as her punishment that she must serve her enemies. Then in Deut 31:16–18:

> Then Yahweh said to Moses: You are about to lie down with your fathers: then this people will rise and play the harlot after the foreign gods of the land into whose midst they are going. And they shall abandon me (*wa'^azabānî*) and break my covenant which I made with them. Then my anger shall be kindled against them and I will abandon them (*wa'^azabtîm*) and hide my face from them; and they shall be devoured. And many evils (*rā'ôt*) and troubles shall come upon them so that they shall say in that day: Is it not because our God is not among us that these evils have come upon us. But I, for my part, will surely hide my face on that day because of all the evil (*hārā'*) which they have done because they turned to other gods.

The Israel that abandons (*'āzab*) Yahweh will be abandoned by him. The evil (*rā'āh*) which she has done brings evils (*rā'ôt*) upon her. In this case we note the evil comes not by the direct action of Yahweh but because he has abandoned the people.

All of the above suggests that at least one possible source or content for the prophetic correspondence of sin and judgment is the curses of the covenantal traditions.[10]

III. A third possible setting or origin for at least some of the correspondence patterns discussed here is provided in the observation of Wolff, Lohfink, and others before and after them that there is a talionic style or way of thinking in the correspondence pattern. We shall seek to develop that observation in relation to some of the texts cited here as well as some of the comparative legal material.

[9] Mays, *Micah*, 143.

[10] Lohfink draws further lines from Hos 4:4–6 to covenantal traditions but these tend to apply particularly to that passage and are less directly applicable.

Claus Westermann has described in detail the prophetic judgment speech in its various formulations and demonstrated convincingly that it has its origins as a type of speech in the legal and judicial activity of Israel.[11] His analysis needs to be expanded or completed with regard to the significance of the conception of the heavenly assembly in relation to the prophet's task and the judicial setting of the judgment speech. The prophet functions as herald or messenger of the council of Yahweh and gains his authority by participation in the council and by authorization of Yahweh to declare his decree. Many of the call narratives or references that are preserved testify to the prophet's place in the heavenly assembly and the significance of that for his message (e.g. Isa 6; Jer 23:18–23; Isa 40; Ezek 1–6; 1 Kgs 22; possibly Amos 3:7). The roles of Yahweh as king, judge, and warrior (roles that can be distinguished and may be accented at particular points but are not always separated) correspond to the functions of the heavenly assembly as royal court, judicial court, and heavenly army.[12] This setting as the context in which Yahweh decides and decrees means that the prophetic identity and role involve related functions. He is the mediator of Yahweh's kingship to the earthly king, proclaimer of Yahweh's judgment for breach of sacral law, and herald of Yahweh's war against Israel or other nations.[13] In these functions appropriate types of speech become the vehicle for the divine word, one of them being the judgment speech. The council of Yahweh, however, and the prophet's function in it provide the necessary link from the legal practices of Israel to the prophet's proclamation of Yahweh's word of judgment. There is no reason for not assuming that Yahweh functions as judge in the court, the one who determines guilt or innocence and announces the verdict and the reason for it.

What is important for our purposes here is that the legal-judicial origins of this type of speech suggest also a similar setting as one of the possible sources for the correspondence pattern. Two passages (Josh 7 and 1 Kgs 20:35ff.) indicate in some fashion a judicial process. In Josh 7 there is a movement from *binding statute*—not to trouble the camp by taking of the *ḥērem*—to *crime*—troubling the camp in this fashion—to *sacral-judicial process* of discovering the guilty one, accusing him of bringing trouble, and announcing the punishment that Yahweh will bring trouble on him, and finally to *execution of the sentence*.

1 Kgs 20:35ff., as we have noted, while not set in an actual judicial context, is formulated entirely in legal and judicial terms: a casuistically formulated requirement with a threat of talionic punishment that uses the explicit

[11] Westermann, *Basic Forms of Prophetic Speech*.

[12] Cf. the similar responsibilities of the divine assembly in Mesopotamian thought as noted by T. Jacobsen, *The Treasures of Darkness*, 87.

[13] F. M. Cross, *Canaanite Myth and Hebrew Epic* (Cambridge: Harvard University Press, 1973) 223–29; and P. D. Miller, "The Divine Council and the Prophetic Call to War," *VT* 18 (1968) 100–107.

formula of talion *x taḥat x* and even includes a compensation clause; declaration of a *mišpāṭ*, a judgment or decision; and a sentence pronounced which refers back to the "statute" and cites the penalty of talion by explicit reference but also with an expansion "people for people" that reflects the movement from formal legal language to prophetic judgment speech. But in this instance we find the precise nominally formed talion formula and not just the repetition of verbs. That is, the judgment speech is a precise case of talion and not merely a general notion of talion. It suggests, however, why talionic notions are found elsewhere in the correspondence pattern. If one includes as a reference for talionic formulations Lev 24:19–20 with the inclusion "as you have done/given, so shall it be done/given to you" (including repetition of action word), then the point of contact between the correspondence pattern and talion becomes much stronger. Such a formulation in P is a very general statement of talionic principle and may be seen as the climax of a long development.[14] But it also indicates an understanding of talion as a religio-legal principle that needs to be included both in describing talion as a juridicial category and in comprehending what the prophets are about as they use the pattern and rhetoric of correspondence. At least two examples of prophetic words of judgment are formulated almost precisely on the Lev 24:19–20 model: *ka'ᵃšer* + verb *kēn* + verb. These are 1 Sam 15:33 and Obad 15b, the latter being the same as Lev 24:19b. Other formulations of correspondence come close to this.

Insofar, however, as one sees one of the sources of the correspondence device in the prophets as *lex* (or *ius*) *talionis*, that must be understood broadly. At times one is dealing with talion in its literal or precise sense. At other times one encounters a variation of talion or an expression of it symbolically as in what are sometimes called "mirror" punishments. This latter category is probably not generally acceptable to jurists as a way of dealing with talion in a legal sense,[15] but an examination of some of the statutes in the legal collections reveals clearly that indeed there are variations on the talion formula that, if not technically related to it, bring one into a similar sphere of meaning. Indeed jurists will sometimes discuss all such laws together in relation to talion.[16] Further, this complexity is reflected in the correspondence motif as it is found in the prophets.

[14] B. S. Jackson, "The Problem of Exodus 21:22–25 (*ius talionis*)," *Essays in Jewish Comparative and Legal History* (Leiden: E. J. Brill, 1975) 107.

[15] Cf. J. Weismann, "Talion und öffentliche Strafe im Mosäischen Rechte," *Um das Prinzip* . . . 337–38, where he points out how such symbolic talion is important for the impression it makes on others. He would not see recompense or retribution in this type of law. Weismann also notes Diodorus Siculus's testimony to the frequency of "mirror" punishments in Egyptian law.

[16] E.g. G. R. Driver and J. Miles, *The Babylonian Laws* (Oxford: Oxford University Press, 1952–55).

When one examines the legal collections to see where some form of talion or correspondence between crime and punishment is present, it is possible to see (three) categories of laws that have a *logical* relationship to each other.

Category 1—General Correspondence

One begins with the common and natural legal movement from offense to restitution or punishment for *that* offense. This is a natural relationship of punishment to a specific offense that is basic to law. The punishment in some fashion reflects, corresponds, is appropriate to the crime. If that is not the case, then both statute and punishment are likely to be challenged. This is characteristic of both civil and criminal law. Some laws show the association of the offense and punishment or restitution more closely than others, but many examples would illustrate the category. One might cite the series of Hittite laws having to do with theft of different animals where the punishment is a restitution in kind (#57ff.)

> #59 If anyone steals a ram, they used to give formerly 30 sheep. Now he shall give 15 sheep, (specifically) 5 ewes, 5 rams (and) 5 lambs.[17]

From the same laws #96–98 have to do with the theft of grain from a granary or setting a house on fire where the granary must be filled and the house restored. CH 42 and 43 deal with failure to cultivate a rented field and demand a payment of grain or plowing of the field and returning it to the owner.

Category 2—Talionic Correspondence

In legal talion formulations the general relationship of punishment to crime becomes very precise and exact. The punishment will be the same as the crime. The wrongdoer will suffer the same injury that his victim did. Obviously such a formulation has only limited applicability in this precise sense. It functions primarily with regard to crimes against the body or person (see Exod 21:23–24; Lev 24:19–20). It does not work as well for other sorts of crimes or illegal acts. It breaks down also when a society has social stratification that affects the severity of punishment and the equation of punishment to crime.

But the principle of talion is already operating to some degree in the examples mentioned in Category 1. Modified forms of it which represent a link between Category 1 and Category 2 are demonstrated by such statutes as CH 219:

> If a physician performed a major operation on a commoner's slave with a bronze lancet and has caused (his) death, he shall make good slave for (*kīma*) slave.[18]

[17] *ANET*, 192.
[18] *ANET*, 175.

or CH 231:

> If it has caused the death of a slave of the owner of the house, so he shall give slave for slave to the owner of the house.[19]

or Exod 21:36:

> Or if it is known that the ox has been accustomed to gore in the past, and its owner has not kept it in, he shall pay ox for (*taḥat*) ox, and the dead beast shall be his.

Here, of course, talion has to do with compensation. But the penalty-punishment component is clearly present in Exod 21:36 when one compares it with v 35 where the oxen are sold and divided between the two owners. The result of both cases is the same—a dead ox. In both cases restitution is related to the problem. But in v 36 where the act has become a matter of criminal negligence, then we have the talion formula, and restitution is combined with penalty.

Strict talion formulations in biblical law are found in Exod 21:23–35; Lev 24:17–21; and Deut 19:21. In the code of Hammurabi we have talionic formulations in 196; 197; and 200:

> 196 If a seignior has destroyed the eye of a member of the aristocracy they shall destroy his eye.
>
> 197 If he has broken a(nother) seignior's bone, they shall break his bone.
>
> 200 If a seignior has knocked out a tooth of a seignior of his own rank, they shall knock out his tooth.[20]

Several examples may also be found in the Middle Assyrian Laws:

> 10 (If) either a seignior or a lady entered a(nother) seignior's (house) and killed (either a man) or a woman (they shall give) the murderers (to the next-of-kin), and if he chooses he may put them to death, or (if he chooses) he may spare (them but) take (their property) . . .
>
> 20 If a seignior lay with his neighbor, when they have prosecuted him (and) convicted him, they shall lie with him (and) turn him into a eunuch.
>
> 52 If a seignior struck a harlot and caused her to have a miscarriage, they shall inflict blow for blow upon him; he shall compensate with a life.[21]

MAL 50 also involves a talion but the law is complex and includes vicarious talion:

> (If a seignior) struck a(nother) seignior's (wife) and caused her to have (a miscarriage) they shall treat (the wife of the seignior), who caused the (other) seignior's wife to (have a miscarriage), as he treated her; he shall compensate for her fetus with a life. However, if that woman died, they shall put the seignior to death; he shall compensate for her fetus with a life. But when that

[19] *ANET*, 176. Cf. Lipit-Ištar Code, #12.

[20] *Ibid.*, 181–85. For detailed discussion of the Middle Assyrian Laws see G. R. Driver and J. Miles, *The Assyrian Laws* (Oxford: Oxford University Press, 1935) and G. Cardascia, *Les lois Assyriennes*, "Litteratures anciennes du Proche-Orient," (Paris: Les Éditions du Cerf, 1969).

[21] *ANET*, 181–85.

> woman's husband has no son, if someone struck her so that she had a miscarriage, they shall put the striker to death; even if her fetus is a girl, he shall compensate with a life.[22]

Further examples of talion as vicarious substitutions are found in both MAL and CH:

> . . . if a seignior took the virgin by force and ravished her, either in the midst of the city or in the open country or at night in the street or in a granary at a city festival, the father of the virgin shall take the wife of the virgin's ravisher and give her to the ravished . . . MAL 55[23]
> If that woman has died, they shall put his daughter to death. CH 210[24]
> If the pledge has died from beating or abuse in the house of his distrainer, the owner of the pledge shall prove it against his merchant, and if it was the seignior's son, they shall put his son to death . . . CH 116[25]
> If it has caused the death of a son of the owner of the house, they shall put the son of that builder to death. CH 231[26]

All of these in one fashion or another portray a strict *lex talionis*. The typical formula in the biblical examples is *x taḥat x* (see Exod 21:23–24; Lev 24:18 and 20). A variant appears in Deut 19:21 *x be- x* . CH has a similar formulation in 219 and 231: *x kīma* (= *taḥat/b^{e}*) *x* .[27] But the *lex talionis* can be expressed in other ways than just *x taḥat/b^{e}x*. As we have remarked earlier, Lev 24:19–20 elaborates the principle with corresponding verbs: *ka'^{a}šer 'āśāh kēn yē'āśeh lô* (v 19 - *'āśāh* repeated) and *ka'^{a}šer yittēn mûm bā'ādām kēn yinnātēn bô* (v 20)—formulations that appear in identical or similar way in 1 Sam 15:33 and Obad 15:[28]

ka'^{a}šer šikk^{e}lāh nāšîm ḥarbekā kēn tiškal minnāšîm 'immekā 1 Sam 15:33
ka'^{a}šer 'āśîtā yē'āśeh lāk Obad 15 (see below).

These formulations in Leviticus which express talion by repeating verbs (*'āśāh*, *nātan*), and thus shift the correspondence from the subject to the action in a way comparable to many of the prophetic judgment speeches, may be secondary expansions in their context but they parallel the way the notion of talion is formulated in several examples from the cuneiform laws cited:

CH 200 crime = knock out (tooth) *nadû(m)*
punishment = knock out (tooth) *nadû(m)*
CH 196 crime = destroy (eye) *ḫuppudu(m)*
punishment = destroy (eye) *ḫuppudu(m)*
CH 197 crime = break (bone) *šabāru(m)*
punishment = break (bone) *šabāru(m)*

[22] *Ibid.*, 184.
[23] *Ibid.*, 185.
[24] *Ibid.*, 175.
[25] *Ibid.*, 170.
[26] *Ibid.*, 176.
[27] Cf. MAL 52.
[28] Cf. Jer 50:15, 29 (with verb *'āśāh*).

In the last three cases we are dealing with the same sort of bodily injury that comes under the rubric of talion in biblical law. But here repeated verbs are used rather than *x* for *x*, although as MAL 52 indicates these could have been formulated on the nominal model. Equally instructive is MAL 20 where the crime is "lying with" (*nâku*) one's neighbor and the punishment is to "lie with" (*nâku*) the offender and make him a eunuch, i.e. castrate him. Even without the sentence "they shall lie with him" the punishment would have been appropriate to the crime. But the somewhat unusual sentence "they shall lie with him" makes the law into a precise talionic one. Technically it belongs with the next category but it overlaps with this one and should be kept in mind when looking at the phenomenon of repeated action words.

These last examples not only tie the prophetic correspondence of crime and punishment more closely to the legal category of talion but they force a modification of Lohfink's view that the examples of verbal correspondence reflect talionic ideas but not talionic style. Both principle and formulation are reflected in the legal expressions of *lex talionis*.

Most of the examples of correspondence in the prophetic judgment speeches involving the same verbs in indictment and announcement of punishment can be related to this talionic category. That includes nearly all of the judgment speeches in narrative settings as well as Hab 2:15–17, Joel 4:4–13; Deut 32:21; Mic 2:1–5; 3:1–4; Hos 4:4–6; Jer 30:16; and Isa 33:1 and 3:11 (on which see final chapter/section).

Category 3

In the third category there is a shift away from talion in a strict sense, and the correlation or correspondence between crime and punishment in the statutes is that the *instrument or means* of the crime is the object of punishment. This is not common in the laws of the Old Testament, the specific example of it being Deut 25:11:

> If men fight with one another and the wife of one of the men draws near to save her husband from the hand of the one who is beating him, and puts out her hand, and seizes him by his private parts, you shall cut off her hand; your eye shall have no pity. (Cf. Matt 5:29–30)

But it appears numerous times in the cuneiform laws:

> If a man's slave-woman, comparing herself to her mistress, speaks insolently to her (or: him), her mouth shall be scoured with 1 quart of salt (Ur-Nammu #22 B 29).[29]

In CH the following examples may be noted:

[29] *ANET*, 525.

192	An adopted son who says to foster-parents: "You are not my mother/father" shall have his tongue cut out.
193	An adopted son who comes to hate foster parents and goes off to parental home shall have his eye plucked out.
194	A wet-nurse who has had a child die in her care and contracts for another without revealing this shall have her breast cut off.
195	A son who strikes his father shall have his hand cut off.
218	A surgeon who causes a man's death or loss of an eye in an operation shall have his hand cut off.
226	A brander who cuts off a slave mark without consent of slave owner shall have his hand cut off.
253	A man who steals the seed or fodder of a man whose lands he is overseeing shall have his hand cut off.[30]

In the Middle Assyrian laws we find among others one comparable to Deut 25:11:

8	A woman crushing a man's testicle in a brawl shall have a finger cut off.
9	A man laying hands on another man's wife shall have a finger cut off. If he has kissed her, they shall draw his lips across the edge of a blade.
15	A spared adulterer is castrated.[31]

Within the prophetic writings there are not many examples of correspondence exactly like these because they are individual and deal with parts of the body, but there are several cases where the instrument or means of the crime is the point where punishment is focused, or the means of punishment, e.g:

Amos 7:16–17	Amaziah is stripped of his priesthood for using it to try to stop the prophetic word.
Hos 10:1–3	The altars and pillars of Israel's sin are destroyed.
2 Sam 12:10a	The sword that killed Uriah will not depart from David's house.
Hos 10:13–15	The sin of trusting in military might leads to destruction of war.
Mic 3:15	The means of prophetic profit-making will be taken away.

Related to the above but somewhat distinguishable from these examples are those cases in legal material and judgment speeches where the punishment seems to have more symbolic force. Two cases that seem to fit such a description are CH 21 and 25:

> If a seignior made a breech in a house, they shall put him to death in front of that breach and wall him in.[32]
> If a fire broke out in a seignior's house and a man who went to extinguish (it) cast his eye on the goods of the owner of the house that man shall be thrown into that fire.[33]

[30] *Ibid.*, 175–76.

[31] *Ibid.*, 181.

[32] *Ibid.*, 167.

[33] *Ibid.* Although I have not seen the text, Driver and Miles cite an order issued by Rim Sin of Larsa to throw into an oven a slave who thrust a fellow slave into a furnace. Driver and Miles, *The Babylonian Laws*, I, 116., n. 6.

In the Middle Assyrian Laws the case (A 40) of the harlot who veils herself in public having hot pitch poured on her head appears also to fall into this category. Correspondence still exists but the expression of it broadens. The walling in of the one who makes the breach in the wall has in itself no punishing force. Nor is it talion. But it dramatizes the crime and correlates the punishment to the crime vividly.[34] So also for the prostitute who is given a veil of pitch whose symbolic force could escape neither offender nor those who view her. One notes further that in all cases the punishment takes on a heightened sense of irony and poetic justice.

It would seem that this category has some analogy to those judgment speeches where the correspondence is symbolic and the locus of the crime becomes the locus of the punishment (1 Kgs 13:1–2 and 1 Kgs 21:17–19). Further one may see in these examples of locus and instrument as the focus of punishment an extension of the talionic principle in a way that pushes toward the various symbolic forms of correspondence in the prophets.

All the above discussion concerning the relationship of the correspondence pattern to cases of *lex talionis* and related laws must not be construed as suggesting that all examples of the correspondence phenomenon are to be traced to this point. It is one possible source along with others mentioned earlier and indeed perhaps should not be totally separated from the covenant curses. But the analysis above tends to support in some detail the conclusions of those who have seen in the correspondence pattern a talionic notion. It goes further than Lohfink in seeing not only the principle or idea as widespread in the examples of correspondence; but even the formulations are frequently styled in some fairly close analogy to talionic laws of one sort or another.

Further, the recognition of the frequency of the correspondence pattern in the prophetic judgment speeches together with the clear indications of a setting in judicial process and talionic legal formulations serves to reinforce and refine Westermann's basic work on this type of speech. The judgment speech of the prophets represents a juridico-legal process in which X person or X people is/are accused and convicted of crimes or breach of covenant and in some instances on the basis of *lex talionis* or some variation—or in the case of covenant transgressions the stipulations and curses of the covenant—sentenced to an appropriate punishment. The decision is rendered by Yahweh, probably in his assembly, and announced by his herald the prophet. In such cases Yahweh can hardly be seen other than functioning in some way as a judge, and the judgment or sentence is—again in some instances at least—according to judicial norms, i.e. those within the context of *lex talionis*. Such conclusions are not without significance for the discussion engendered by Koch on retribution, on which see the concluding chapter.

[34] See n. 15 above.

CHAPTER III

A Classification of the Patterns of Correspondence

The attempt to categorize the various ways in which the correspondence of sin and judgment is expressed in the prophets must acknowledge a certain artificiality in light of the great variety and individuality of the texts. Nevertheless similarities do exist. Even as various passages may have in common the same genre, so they may also share particular elements within that genre and formulate them in a similar way. The value of some sort of typology or classification is that it enables one to see the larger picture of how the prophets relate sin and judgment and perceive the primary rhetorical devices for doing this. While the line between content and style is rather fuzzy and one cannot describe the one for very long without getting into the other, it is possible to classify the patterns to some degree along these lines in order to see both *what* is being said and *how* it is said. Any particular example may fall into several categories rather than just one. Experimentation with different arrangements suggests that the following schema best conveys the inter-relationships and the most obvious categories:[1]

Classification with primary attention to *talionic* features.

Classification with primary attention to *meaning* and *content*.

Classification with primary attention to *stylistic* features.

I. Classification with primary attention to *talionic* features.

As the previous chapter has demonstrated, a large number of examples express the notion of talion and not infrequently in the explicit style of the talionic formulas.

A. Nominal form = *X taḥat/b^{e} X*

1 Kgs 20:42 is the only explicit example of this formula in the prophetic judgment speeches. It is against an individual king but includes the people:

napš^{e}kā taḥat napšô, ʿamm^{e}kā taḥat ʿammô.

[1] Wolff offers a classification of this phenomenon in his study of the reasons for the prophetic salvation and judgment speeches. He gives several categories based on content but has only one or two examples in each category. He then treats "inner-stylistic" modes of correspondence, describing several ways in which repetition of words creates the correspondence (again with a single example in each case) and mentioning also the use of figures of speech. See "Die Begründungen der prophetischen Heils und Unheilssprüche," 21–28.

B. *ka'ᵃšer* + verb (= sin) . . . *kēn* + verb (= punishment)

1 Sam 15:33: *ka'ᵃšer šikkᵉlāh nāšîm ḥarbekā* (=crime)
kēn tiškal minnāšîm 'immekā (=punishment)

Obad 15–16: *ka'ᵃšer 'āśîtā* (=crime) *yē'āśeh lāk* (=punishment)
ka'ᵃšer šātîtem (=crime)
yištû (=punishment)

[Judg 1:7: *ka'ᵃšer 'āśîtî* (=crime)
kēn šillam lî 'ᵉlōhîm (=punishment)]

Ezek 35:14–15: *kᵉśimḥatᵉkā . . . kēn 'e'ᵉśeh-lāk*

C. Verbs describing punishment are the same as verbs describing crime

1. Complete correspondence (involving three or more elements)

Deut 32:21:

First correspondence:

(Pronoun (*hēm*) + verb (*qin'ûnî*) +
(prep. phrase (*bᵉlō'-'ēl*) =crime
(Pron. (*'anî*) + verb (*'aqnî'ēm*) +
(prep. phrase (*bᵉlō'-'am*) =punishment

Second correspondence:

Verb (*ki'asûnî*) + prep. phrase (*bᵉhablêhem*) =crime
Verb (*'ak'isēm*) + prep phrase (*bᵉgôy nābāl*) =punishment

1 Kgs 21:19: Place (*bimqôm*) + verb (*lāqᵉqû*) + subj. (*hakkᵉlābîm*) + object (*dam nābôt*) = crime
Place (*bimqôm*) + verb (*yālōqqû*) + subj. (*hakkᵉlābîm*) + object (*dāmᵉkā*) = punishment

Ezek 36:6–7: *kᵉlimat gôyim nᵉśā'tem* = crime *haggôyim kᵉlimātām yiśśa'û* = punishment

Joel 4:4–8: A sells B to C, a far-off place (*mākar*)
B sells A to D, a far-off nation (*mākar*)

2. Repetition of key verb(s)

Hos 4:4–6: (*kāšal*), *dāmāh*, *mā'as*, *šākaḥ*

Hos 8:1–6: *zānāh*

Mic 2:1–5: *ḥāšab* + *ra'*

1 Sam 15:10–31: *mā'as*

2 Sam 12:10–11: *lāqaḥ* + object (*'iššāh/nāšîm*)

Hab 2:6b–8a: *šālal* + obj. *gôyim rabbîm*
šālal + subj. *yeter 'ammîm*

Isa 33:1: *šādad*, *bāgad*

Josh 7:25: *'ākar*

Jer 30:16a: *'ākal*
1 Sam 2:30 & 3:13: *qillēl*
Jer 23:1–4: *lō' pāqad/ /pāqad* (inversion)

D. Talionic idea/thought without formulas or repetition of verbs.
Mic 3:1–5: metaphor of cannibalism with repeated nouns but different verbs.
Hab 2:15–16: metaphor of drinking to drunkenness and exposing one's nakedness (*šātāh/ /šāqāh*)
Jer 30:16b: *šō'sayik limšissāh*
(your spoilers become spoil) verb/ /noun
(same root) *bōz^{e}zayik lābaz*
(those preying on you become prey) verb/ /noun (same root)

E. Indirect Correspondence
The examples listed here may be related to Category 3 in the preceding chapter. They involve so-called "mirror" punishments or, more particularly, correspondence that focuses upon instrument, office, locus, or intention-result.

1. *Instrument*
Amos 7:16–17: Amaziah's priesthood as the instrument of his sin becomes the instrument of his punishment. This belongs more obviously and specifically under 2 below.
Hos 10:1–2: The altars and pillars whereby Israel sins are also the objects of destruction as her punishment. Cf. 3 below.
Hos 10:13–15: Although the chariots and warriors in which Israel trusts are not mentioned in the punishment, it is clearly punishment by the instruments of war.
Isa 3:16–4:1: The sin of the women is carried out and manifest by their physical appearance and dress. That becomes then the means of punishment.
Mic 1:7: The harlot's hires which are the instruments of Samaria's sins are at least symbolically the instruments of their judgment.
Mic 3:5–7: The means by which the prophets secure their gain—divination, the divine word—are taken away from them.
2 Sam 12:7–15: The sword of David's sin against Uriah, i.e. the instrument of war, will perpetually harass the Davidic house.
1 Kgs 13:1ff.: Although this belongs more properly under 3, the instrument of Israel's sin, the altar of Bethel, will be the place and instrument of judgment.

While in some of the above cases key words focus the correspondence (e.g. altars and pillars in Hos 10:1–2; harlot's hire in Mic 1:7), sword in

2 Sam 1–2, none of these cases depends upon repetition of key verbs, and repetition in general is not the primary basis for correspondence.

2. *Office*

In all of these cases because the sin is a sin of office, the office is affected either by being taken away (Amos 7:16–17; Hos 4:4–6; Mic 3:5–7; 1 Sam 15:10:31), or by being endangered (2 Sam 12:7–15).

Amos 7:16–17 (priest)
Hos 4:4–5 (priest)
Mic 3:5–7 (prophet)
1 Sam 15:10–31 (king)
2 Sam 12:7–15 (king)
1 Kgs 21:17–19 (king) This is only an implicit case of correspondence of office in that Ahab's usurpation of power leads to his death and thus removal from office. So also probably Jer 14:14.

It should be noted that not every case of the sinful performance of one's office leads to a punishment corresponding to the office (e.g. 1 Sam 2:27–36).

3. *Locus*

The correspondence in several cases has to do with the place where the sin takes place. Here of course the correspondence is symbolic, but like the above examples it sharply focuses attention upon the sin:

Hos 4:1–3 (the *land* is locus of sin and punishment)
Hos 10:1–2 (altars and pillars [see E.1 above])
Mic 3:9–12 (Zion and Jerusalem)
1 Kgs 13:1–2 ("*bimqôm* where the dogs licked up Naboth's blood shall the dogs also lick up your blood" [Jezreel, site of Naboth's vineyard, cf. v 23], 2 Kgs 9:25–26, 30–37).
Ezek 27 (in the heart of the seas)

4. *Result* or *intention*

On this type of correspondence see the discussion of its possible origin in the futility curses of treaty and covenant. The judgment is worked out in terms of the intended result of the sin.

Amos 5:7, 10–11: houses and vineyards
Hos 4:7–10: eating and fertility
Mic 2:1–5: fields
Mic 3:9–12: Zion and Jerusalem
Isa 5:8–10: houses and field (produce of fields)
Isa 30:1–5: refuge
Isa 31:1–3: help
Isa 30:15–17: flight and safety

1 Sam 2:27–38: eating
2 Sam 12:7–15: son born of sin dies

In all of these examples either the intended result is frustrated or the accomplished result taken away.

F. *Non-talionic correspondence*

It should be noted that a number of instances of correspondence do not manifest the style or idea of talion. Because of the importance of this idea in the correspondence of sin and judgment it is necessary to point to the exceptions. In many if not most instances there is reversal of circumstances and a strong sense of irony. One encounters here not infrequently a genuine "poetic justice" in that it is created by the artifice of the poet-prophet, i.e. by means of figures of speech—metaphor, simile, paranomasia. Examples of these are:

Isa 1:21–26
1:29–30
7:9
8:5–8
28:1–4
28:14–18
28:7–13
29:1–3
30:15–17
Jer 5:12–17
14:13–16
Hos 2
7:11–12
Amos 6:1–7
Mic 1:7
7:4

II. Classification with primary attention to *meaning* and *content*

Clearly the preceding category focuses on meaning and content to some degree as well as style. But there are other important groupings that accent content dimensions rather than style and uncover aspects of correspondence of a quite different sort than those relating to talion. Among those that seem the clearest and have at least two examples are the following:

A. The victim of the sin brings about the judgment on the sinner.
Deut 32:21
Hab 2:6b–8
Joel 4:4–8

B. What one did not think would happen does happen.
Isa 28:14–18
30:1–5
30:15–17

31:1–3
Jer 5:12–17
14:13–16
Mic 3:9–12

C. Correspondence is related to sin, judgment, *and salvation.*
Isa 1:21–26
28:1–4
Jer 23:1–4
Hos 2:4ff.

D. A more general principle or theological statement of correspondence is included or related to the specific example.
Jer 14:13–16 (Verse 16b)
Hos 4:7–10 (Verse 9)
8:1–6 (Verse 7)
10:13–15 (Verse 13a)
Joel 4:4–8 (Verses 4 and 7)
Obad 15
Judg 1:7

A subsidiary category consists of those instances where divine *rā'(āh)* is the judgment for human *ra'(ah)*:
2 Sam 12:7–15
1 Kgs 21:17–19 and 20–24
Isa 31:1–3
Mic 2:1–5

Without a specific example of correspondence:
1 Kgs 14:7–16
2 Kgs 21:10–15
Jer 11:17
18:7ff.
23:10–12
26:3

III. Classification with primary attention to *stylistic* features

A. Repetition of *words*

1. Verbs—see the lists in I.B and C and add the following:
Isa 28:14–18 (*šôṭēp*)
29:1–3 (*ḥānāh*)
30:15–17 (*nûs*)

2. Other words (subject, object, prepositional phrase)
1 Sam 2:27–36 (*mā'ôn*)
Isa 1:29–30 (*'ayel/'ēlāh, gannāh*)
5:8–10 (*bêt*)
8:5–8 (*mayim*)
28:1–4 (*'ᵃṭeret, gē'ût, šikrê 'epraim*)
(*ṣîṣ nōbēl ṣᵉbî tip'eret*)

28:7–13 (*ṣaw leṣaw, qaw leqaw*)
28:14–18 (*berît 'et māwet, ḥōzeh/ḥāzût 'et še'ôl, maḥseh kāzāb*, and the root *str*)
30:1–5 (*mā'ôz par'ōh, ḥesôt/ḥāsût beṣēl miṣrayim*)
Jer 5:12–17 (*dābār*)
14:13–16 (*ḥereb* and *rā'āb*)
Ezek 35 (*šmm*)
Ezek 27–28 (*beleb yammîm*)
Hos 10:1–2 (*mizbeḥôt* and *maṣṣēbôt*)
Mic 2:1–5 (*śādôt*)
3:1–4 (*'ôr, še'ēr, 'aṣmôt*)

In some of these cases what happens is that the key word has a positive meaning but it is modified in the judgment so that it is turned into a negative punishment:

Isa 8:5–8 - water
28:14–18 - shelter, refuge
30:1–5 - protection of Pharaoh, refuge in the shade of Egypt
31:1–3 - help

In all of these cases the force of this reversal or the nature of it is due to the nature of the sin—seeking refuge, help, protection, water (of life) somewhere else than in Yahweh.

3. Thematic words

There are three cases where by repetition at least three times a word may be regarded as thematic.

Josh 7:25 (*'ākar*)
Hos 4:1–3 (*'ereṣ*)
Mic 1:7 (*'etnān*)

B. Figures of speech

1. Simile.

Isa 1:29–30 - oak/terebinth, garden
28:1–4 - first ripe fig
30:17 - flagstaff, signal

2. Metaphor.

a. Simple.

Isa 1:19–20 - eating (with the sword)
1:21–26 - purifying of metals
1:31 - fire
8:5–8 - flood
28:14–18 - flood
29:1–3 - siege
Hos 4:7–10 - harlotry
7:11–12 - fowl and fowler
Mic 3:1–4 - cannibalism

b. Extended or multiple metaphor.

Isa 28:1–4 - proud crown trodden under foot
fading flower

Hos 2 - harlotry (cf. Ezek 16 and 23)

Hab 2:15–16 - drinking to drunkenness and
exposing one's nakedness

3. Wordplay.

Deut 32:21 (*lō' 'ēl/lō' 'am* and *hebel/nābāl*

Josh 7:25 (*'ākān/'ākōr/'ākar*)

Isa 1:19–20 (*tō'bû-ṭôb*)

7:9

7:9 (*lō'tā'* (*lō'tā'^{a}mînû/lō'tē'āmēnû*)

30:15–17 (*nûs/nēs*)

Jer 23:1–2 (*rō'îm/rōa'*)

Hos 10:1–2 (only in indictment *rôb/hirbāh; ṭôb/hēṭîbû*)

4:7–9 (*k^{e}rubām/k^{e}bôdām?*)

Amos 6:1–7 (*rēšît haggoyîm/rōš gōlîm*)

Mic 7:4 (*m^{e}sûkah/m^{e}bûkah*)

C. Correspondence via common idea or subject without repetition or figure of speech.

2 Sam 12:7–15 (kingship)

Isa 3:16–4:1 (dress and bearing)

5:8–10 (fields non-productive)

Hos 10:13–15 (war)

Amos 5:7, 10–11 (houses and vineyards non-productive)

Mic 3:5–7 (prophetic revelations)

D. Correspondence worked out in surrounding narrative.

Josh 7

1 Sam 2:27–36

1 Sam 15:10–31

2 Sam 12:7–15

1 Kgs 13:1–2

1 Kgs 21:17–19

It is not possible to summarize the results of such classification completely. One is immediately aware of both patterns and diversity. Various aspects of talionic thinking and formulation are clearly there and play a dominant role but by no means do they exhaust the uses of correspondence. Where wordplay, metaphor, and other figures of speech are the vehicle (cf. especially Isaiah), talion rarely is involved (Mic 3:1–4 and Hab 2:15–16 are exceptions). One notes further that there are several blocks of material where this phenomenon tends to cluster (e.g. Isa 1:28–31; Hos 4; Mic 3; Hab 2, etc.)

The rhetorical possibilities are numerous according to this classification. A repeated word, a play on a word, an elaborated metaphor, reversal of devices were available and used by the prophets to convey a true poetic justice. The multiple ways in which the correlation of sin and punishment was announced confirm the sense of the preceding chapter that this pattern had various roots and reflected several settings rather than being the product of a single origin.

CHAPTER IV

The Judgment of God

This study would not be complete without some reflection on the theology of judgment encountered in the Old Testament in the light of these passages which manifest correlation between sin and judgment. The expression "theology of judgment" is not in this case meant to imply a single, relatively monolithic notion or conception of judgment. On the contrary, the investigation in these pages, though a limited one, suggests a multi-faceted or multi-dimensional perception of the nature and meaning of Israel's experience of judgment. One's sense of that complexity would grow if one moved into the many other passages that do not come into the scope of this investigation. There would be a greater sense of the possibility of God's judgment without any explicit attempt to see the judgment as corresponding in some pointed way to the sin. The passages dealt with here show how widespread such correspondence is and serve to emphasize the role of that correlation in the prophetic notions of judgment. But many passages do not demonstrate such correspondence. It is only those that do which form the basis for the following discussion.

Although it is not our intention (nor indeed our result!) to resolve the issues about judgment and retribution raised by Klaus Koch in his now famous article and debated in response to him, one cannot avoid them in treating the subject of judgment in the Old Testament, especially inasmuch as the texts under study by their very nature force the question when one moves beyond stylistic, rhetorical, or formal consideration to questions of meaning and relationships. Before seeking to draw some conclusions or lines of direction in this regard and as part of that process, it is necessary to look in more detail at some texts not yet taken up or touched on only tangentially. These are prophetic sayings wherein it appears as if some rather general or theological principle of correspondence is set forth. The definition of a "general principle" in this case will not be debated. Others might not categorize the following passages that way, or they might include others in such a category. The ones that follow appear to extrapolate from or impose upon the illustrative examples some more general understanding of what is going on. At a minimum one must include them because they have arisen in the investigation and relate in some fashion to the phenomenon of correspondence or correlation.

I. *Theological Principles Correlating Sin and Judgment*

Hos 4:9 It will be like people, like priests;
and I will visit (*pāqad*) upon him his ways,
and his deeds I will bring back (*hēšîb*) upon him.

This example appears in the context of the elaborated correspondence of vv 4–6 and 7–9. Koch, Wolff, and Mays see this as an example of the *Tun-Ergehen* sphere. There is indeed some sense of that. But the principle being articulated here ***in its context*** is more one of *correspondence* than of *consequence*, though the latter dimension is involved.

(a) The verse begins with a *comparison correspondence* "like people, like priest," which means the priest is being compared to the people or more particularly the fate of the priest will in some way be like that of the people.[1] It is somewhat talionic in the sense "as he has done shall be done to him," though in this case it does not stay as a strictly talionic idea.
(b) The singular pronouns of v 9b refer back to the priest in 9a.
(c) This whole lawsuit against the priest from v 4 on is couched in terms of correspondence. Verses 5 and 6 describe what the priests have brought upon the people: stumbling, destruction, lack of knowledge, and forgetting the law. The verses also say that what they have done will be done to them, i.e. "like people, like priest."
(d) Verse 9b, therefore, is indicating that his judgment will be like his sin, not just that the sin works itself out to the inevitable consequences, which certainly do not have to be like what the sin is or what the priests have done to the people.
(e) That a strict correspondence is not all that is meant is indicated by v 10 where a correspondence is indicated but it is of the futility curse notion—frustration of the result or intention of the sin.

This understanding of Hos 4:9 is confirmed in 12:3. Apart from Hos 2:4 this verse contains the only other usage of *rîb* in Hosea outside of the three uses in Hos 4:1ff. Kinship with that chapter and sequence of related passages is found in this verse also, which precisely parallels the construction in 4:9b except in one regard. Both are as follows:

pāqad + (*ᶜal* + suffix) + (*dᵉrākîm*)//
(*maᶜᵃlatîm* + suffix) + *hēšîb* + (*lᵉ* + suffix)

In both cases, Yahweh is the subject, once in first person (4:9b) and once in third person (12:3). The significant difference is that both *dᵉrākîm* and *maᶜᵃlātîm* are preceded by the preposition *kᵉ*- = "as, according to." The punishment that comes is *the like* of the sin[2] not primarily the consequence of the sin. It is that correspondence between sin and judgment that the dual *kᵉ*- intends to express and it should be kept in mind that the notion of correspondence is in no sense inherent in the notion of a deed working out its

[1] Cf. BDB, 454 and the expression "like father like son" where the latter is being compared to the former.

[2] See BDB on *kᵉ*-.

consequences with an intrinsic relation between the two, the one an outgrowth of the other. Trusting in a foreign power may lead to foreign domination and oppression or destruction. But the consequence is not *the like* of the prior action. Indeed Isaiah has to work out correspondences depending on wordplay and metaphors to express the relation between the sin of trusting in a foreign power and Yahweh's judgment of that because the punishment is not like the deed.

While, therefore, the notion of the fate-effecting deed may be carried by the use of the Hiphil of *šûb* and possibly by *pāqad* + *ᶜal*, it does not seem that the primary intention of this theological principle is to express that. Rather the prophet affirms a relation of *correspondence* as much or more than one of consequence or result between the human deed and the divine response.

Hosea 8:7

Koch has pointed to the frequent use of the metaphor of sowing and reaping in Hosea as an indicator of the *Tun-Ergehen* sequence. Certainly that image points to the connection between deed and result probably as clearly as any other image. Once, again, however, the imagery seems to express the notion of correspondence between sin and judgment as much as it does the consequential relationship, i.e. what is reaped is like what is sown. It is not just that a small seed is sown and a process set in motion which yields a full fruit. The expressions for sowing and reaping stand in parallelism, suggesting essentially that what you sow is what you will reap. Hos 8:7 reads

> *kî rûaḥ yizrāʿû*
> *wᵉsûpātāh yiqṣōrû*
> For they sow the wind
> and reap the whirlwind.

These are parallel expressions to denote the correspondence of sin and punishment. *rûaḥ* and *sûpāh* are parallel words referring to the same thing (cf. Isa 17:13 and Job 21:18). Either word is also interchangeable with *saᶜar* and *sᵉᶜārāh*. The figure bears some resemblance to 12:1:

> Ephraim shepherds the wind
> and pursues the east wind all day long.

Chapter 8:7 may have in mind also a single notion, i.e. Ephraim is creating or dealing with a tempest. Or it may be a double-sided notion, i.e. Israel gets what she gives. But if it is the latter, the concern is as much to express the correspondence of sin and judgment as it is to express how judgment comes about.

Hosea 10:12–13

A positive example of the sowing-reaping imagery appears in 10:12.

Sow for yourselves righteousness;
Reap according to steadfast love;
Break up your fallow ground.

Here the arrangement of parallel clauses indicates that the prophet is not thinking only or necessarily primarily of a sequential movement and a careful process of the deed that sets loose a result. What is sown is parallel to what is reaped. The prophet calls for Israel to deal in *ṣᵉdāqāh*, that is *ḥesed*. As in 8:7 the verse may either express one notion with three clauses, or it may point to a correspondence of good deed and positive result. But it does not seem to manifest an interest in using the imagery to express with some care the idea of the fate-effecting deed. If so, how would one explain the placement of the third clause, which, as the somewhat parallel expression in Jer 4:3 shows, ought to come at the beginning of the sequence. One observes further that the emphasis on correspondence is underscored also with the use of *lᵉpî*—"according to" steadfast love. Implicit in the expression as in the parallelism of *ṣᵉdāqāh* and *ḥesed* is the idea that what one gets should be like what one gives. At least the passage seems to have more of that nuance at its center than the concern to express that what one gets works itself out of what one gives. I would see the basic intent and meaning of the verse in the single and familiar prophetic call to do righteousness, which, as Amos recognized as well as Hosea, is the way in which one "seeks Yahweh."

The correspondence continues in the latter half of the verse to indicate that Israel's sowing of *ṣᵉdāqāh* for themselves (*lākem*) will be met by Yahweh's raining *ṣᵉdāqāh* for them (*lākem*).

Hosea 10:13

The sowing and reaping imagery in Hosea continues in v 13 and expresses somewhat more directly the notion of *Tun-Ergehen* as Koch described it:

You have plowed wickedness (*reša'*);
you have reaped injustice (*'awlātāh*);
you have eaten the fruit of lies (*pᵉrî kāḥaš*).

Particularly with the reference to eating the fruit of lies and the sequence plowing, reaping, and eating one sees some indication of the relationship of the wicked deed that leads to or brings about a negative consequence. But that interpretation, which does seem to grow out of the text, is not without problems. For one thing the verbs are all here in the perfect indicating past action. That is true of the verbs for reaping and eating as well as plowing. One would expect the former to indicate future action growing out of the present act of plowing wickedness. One recognizes, however, that the verbs in verses 14ff. also may point to judgment as a past act. More serious as a problem for reading this as a sequence of *Tun-Ergehen* is the use of the word *'awlātāh* in the second colon to indicate what Ephraim has reaped. While Koch is correct that some words can refer to both crime and punishment, sin and judgment,[3] the root *'wl* in any of its forms is not such a word. It always refers to acts of injustice or iniquity and never to calamitous events or consequences or punishment in the way that such words as *'āwōn*, *'āwen*, or *ra'* can. In several contexts it is explicitly stated that God never does *'āwel* or *'awlāh* (Deut 32:4; Job 34:10; Ps 91:16; 2 Chr 19:7). Proverbs 22:8 expresses quite well the notion of the deed that effects its consequence, referring to *'awlāh*, but here *'awlāh* is clearly the negative human act and the resultant calamity is indicated by *'āwen*, which certainly can refer to trouble as an effect as well as evil as a cause:

> Whoever sows injustice will reap calamity.

But it is just this kind of sentence that one would expect in Hos 10:13—if it conforms to Koch's analysis of the *Tun-Ergehen* relation—that in fact is not present in that verse. Iniquity is reaped, not calamity. Once again one suspects that this verse, as possibly 8:7 and 10:12, expresses a single notion, i.e., you have engaged in injustice (sowing, reaping, eating) rather than two notions or a double-sided one, to wit: You have engaged in injustice which has inevitably led (or will lead) to the result that you have suffered calamity.

Hosea 7:2

The sense of the *Tun-Ergehen Zusammenhang* as Koch and others have described it is probably most clearly manifest in Hosea in 7:2 (cited by Koch):

> But they do not consider
> that I remember all their evil.
> Now their deeds surround them;
> they are before my face.

The second line conveys through battle imagery the sense of the deeds effecting disastrous consequences. The wicked deeds of the people now surround them like a military siege and will eventually bring about their destruction.[4] One notes that this image is balanced by a reference to Yahweh's knowledge of the deeds and his judgment on them. As Koch has pointed out, Yahweh is the one who watches over, sets in power, and accomplishes or completes the connection between the deeds and their outcome or "fate," to use Koch's term.

[3] Koch, *Um das Prinzip der Vergeltung*, 433.

[4] Cf. *sabab* in Pss 18:6; 22:13, 17; 49:6; 88:18; 118:10–12.

Jeremiah

When one looks at The Book of Jeremiah for theological statements or principles about the relationship between sin and judgment one finds notions both of consequence and of correspondence. In some cases as in Hosea they come together in a way that makes it difficult to talk about them separately. There are several passages that convey clearly the conception of the "destiny-producing deed," i.e., judgment understood as the fate brought about by the human deeds set in motion. Two examples may be cited in Jer 2.

> What iniquity did your fathers find in me
> that they went far from me,
> and went after worthlessness (*hāhebel*)
> and became worthless (*wayyehbāhlû*) (2:5)?[5]

Koch properly sees here an illustration of the notion that a deed brings about a result that may be rooted inevitably in some sense in the deed so that a clear connection can be seen between the two. Going after *hebel* leads to becoming *hebel*. Equally important for our consideration is that the prophet seeks to heighten that relationship and one's perception of it by use of the rhetoric of correspondence. The correspondence, of course, is in the repetition of the root *hbl*, first as a noun and then as a verb. It also involves a play on words because *hebel* is virtually a technical term in Jeremiah and used also in Dtr for idols (Jer 8:19; 10:3, 8, 15 = 51:18; 14:22; 16:19; 1 Kgs 16:13, 22; 2 Kgs 17:15). In Jer 10:2–10 the prophet explains in some detail why the idols may be considered as *hebel*. They cannot move, speak, walk, do evil, or do anything else for that matter. They are as empty, as unsubstantial as *hebel*. The result of this pursuit of the worthless, vain idols was that the fathers became as unsubstantial and worthless as what they pursued. This is not technically a formulation of punishment. Indeed it is further manifestation of their sin. But it is a consequence of their sin that corresponds to the sin.

2:19

In this same chapter verse 19 expresses the *Tun-Ergehen* connection in a manner reminiscent of Hos 7:2.

> Your wickedness (*rāʿāh*) shall chastise you (*tᵉyassᵉrēk*);
> and your apostasy shall reprove you.

The verb *yāsar* appears a number of times in Jeremiah, but in verbal and nominal forms it always has a personal subject who is always Yahweh. It refers to Yahweh's activity to discipline and instruct Judah, a judging activity

[5] This is not strictly a theological statement or principle in the manner of the other examples discussed here. I include it because it is one of the passages to which Koch refers (435, n. 5).

whereby the Lord seeks to change the ways of the people. Here the subject of the chastening action is *rāʿātēk* "your wickedness." Judah's wickedness and apostasy will have consequences that will serve to chastise, correct and judge her. The inner connection of act and consequence is sharply underscored. That does not mean that Yahweh is uninvolved in the process. On the contrary Jeremiah has numerous references to Yahweh's chastisement of the people (2:30; 5:3; 7:28; 10:24; 30:11; 31:18 (17); 47:28, etc.). As Koch has made clear, Yahweh is seen as the one who sets the connection between act and consequence in force. Such is the case here. There is nothing contradictory between 2:19 and the several references to the Lord's chastening activity.

6:19

The interaction of the divine activity and the fate-effecting deed is nowhere better seen than in 6:19.

> Hear, O earth,
> behold I am bringing evil upon this people,
> and fruit of their devices.

The *rāʿāh* that will happen to the people is the consequence of their own wicked plans and schemes. The fruit of *rāʿāh* is *rāʿāh*, i.e., the *deed-consequence* connection. But the passage is equally clear that the one who brings about that connection, who sees that *rāʿāh* brings forth a similar or corresponding fruit is Yahweh. He sets the relationship into effect and brings it to completion. One has to be careful about referring to inevitable or irrevocable consequences of human deeds of good or evil without recognizing how thoroughly Israel understood the relationship being guided by the word of God.

14:16

Yet another passage in Jeremiah expresses the dual character of human actions and the judgment of God. The unit 14:13–16 discussed earlier concludes with the words:

> For I will pour out their wickedness (*rāʿātām*) upon them (v 16).

What is the *rāʿah* here? Is it the wickedness of the people or the fate they will suffer? It is both. As we have already noted *raʿ/rāʿāh* can be human evil or divine judgment. Therein is the correspondence as well as the consequence. *rāʿāh* leads to *rāʿāh*. One can understand that purely as the connection between a deed and its consequences. And indeed the passage affirms that connection. But it also declares that the correspondence and consequence are brought about by Yahweh who sees that their evil deeds will bring about a correspondingly evil fate.

21:14

Again both consequence and correspondence of evil deeds are indicated in the judgment God will bring:

> I will punish you (*pāqad* + *'al* + suffix)
> *according to* the fruit of all your deeds.

The reference to "the fruit" of their deeds suggests the connection between deed and effect as the process of judgment but the primary thrust of the prophetic word seems to be the correlation between what they have done, its evil effects, and what will be done to them, i.e., the same sort of evil effects. It is not that Yahweh punishes *with* the fruit of their deeds, but *according to, the like* of their deeds (17:10 and 32:19). What *ma'allêkem* are is indicated both by the immediate context (v 12—injustice, oppression, robbery) and by the larger context of Jeremiah. When Jeremiah says to the people: "Amend your ways (*darkêkem*) and your deeds (*ma^{e}allêkem*)" (7:3,5), he explicitly spells out what those deeds are: murder, adultery, swearing falsely, burning incense to Baal, going after other gods (7:9). He also indicates by inference what their deeds are in his injunctions to execute justice, not to oppress the weak or shed innocent blood (7:5–6). Yahweh will punish Judah in a manner or in a degree corresponding to or equivalent to the fruit of such deeds. The people's "ways" and "deeds" are regularly spoken of as "evil" (*rōa'*, *ra'*, *rā'āh*), for example Jer 25:5; 33:15; 21:12; 11:18; 23:22. With such terminology we encounter the theological principle of correspondence mentioned earlier which is prominent in both Jeremiah and the Deuteronomistic historian. That is the understanding that *ra'* (*rā'āh*) i.e. human wickedness, leads to *ra'* (*rā'āh*), i.e. divine punishment. They are parts of a whole and the diagram *ra'* ⟶*ra'* conveys simply and sharply both the *deed-effect connection* that Koch has discerned and the emphasis upon the correspondence that we are underscoring here. *Ra'* in some sense inevitably brings about *ra'*. Indeed the *ra'* is one and not two separate and unrelated events. At the same time the texts clearly speak of Yahweh bringing upon the people (*hēbî' 'el/ 'al*) *ra'* because of their *ra'*. Yet this free divine decision or action is still seen as a kind of inevitable consequence of their ways and deeds. And the notion of *ra'* points to the clear correlation of sin and punishment in that the people experience as judgment something of the same sort as they brought about or did in their sin. Indeed all the particular sins denounced and the particular examples of a corresponding punishment announced are manifestations of this large theological principle that *ra'* leads to *ra'*. One can see, for example, as we have noted, the *ra'* that grows out of David's *ra'* with Bathsheba and against Uriah. And it is clearly *ra'* of the same character as that in which David engaged. Consequence and correspondence between sin and judgment are caught up in the *ra'* that is both human action and divine response.

50:15 (cf. v 29)

In the oracles against the nations in Jeremiah there occurs a theological statement of the correspondence between sin and punishment that is talionic in its form:

> For this is the vengeance of the Lord (*niqmat yhwh*);
> take vengeance upon her,
> do to her as she has done (*ka'ᵃšer 'āśᵉtā 'ᵃśû lāh*).

The formulation of the last line is similar to Lev 24:19 (cf. Judg 6:1,7). The Lord announces against Babylon the judgment of talion. Her punishment will be like her sin (cf. v 14). What she has done to other nations (siege, death, destruction of city and inhabitants, exile) will be done to her. This is the action or judgment of Yahweh but it is wrought out through the agency of the other nations (v 9). The vengeance (*nᵉqāmāh*) of Yahweh is that talion will be executed against Babylon through the processes of history (cf. 51:6). In those processes one can expect and point to the relationship between sin and judgment as both correspondence and consequence.

Isaiah 3:9b–11

There are other passages in the prophets comparable to these. We shall refer only to three more that follow along much the same lines as the passages in Jeremiah above. Isa 3:9b–11 conveys the complex relationship between sin and judgment that we have seen there.[6]

> 9b . . . Woe to them!
> for they do (*gāmᵉlû*) to themselves evil (*rā'āh*).
> 10 Say to the righteous: How good! (*kî ṭôb*)
> for they eat the fruit of their deeds (*ma'allêhem*).
> 11 Woe to the wicked! Evil! (*rā'āh*)
> for the work of his hands (*gᵉmûl yādāyw*) shall be
> done to him.

One observes again the category of *rā'āh* (*ra'*) as a way of describing both the wickedness that the wicked do (v 9) and their fate of doom and evil (vv 9 and 11), even as *ṭob* characterizes the deeds and the reward of the righteous. The root *gml* appears here in nominal and verbal forms as it does in a number of passages that have to do with the question of retribution. The words from this root rarely mean in themselves recompense. They refer to what one has done to someone or rendered to someone. In context they may have to do with requital and the context can give a positive or negative character to the *gᵉmûl (āh)*. Here in 9 and 11 *gāmal* and *gᵉmûl* refer to the evil deeds of the wicked, but the conception of the fate-effecting deed is

[6] For detailed textual discussion see W. L. Holladay, "Isa III 10–11: an Archaic Wisdom Passage," *VT* 18 (1968) 481–87.

strongly suggested in verse 9b. The evil they do (their sin), they do to themselves (the consequence of their *g^{e}mûl* which is brought about out of their wickedness).

This connection between deed and the fate it brings about is sharpened into a more retributional notion in verse 11 with the correspondence between sin and judgment expressed in nearly talionic form. The consequence grows out of the deed but it is also the same as the deed. Again the *g^{e}mûl* is one and the same.

Obad 15–16

The announcement of the day of the Lord against the nations in Obad 15ff. characterizes the punishment of the nations in strict talionic fashion:

15 For the day of the Lord is near
  upon all the nations.
As you have done it shall be done to you;
  your deeds (*g^{e}mulkā*) shall return on your head.
16 For as you drank on my holy mountain,
  all the nations shall drink continuously;
they shall drink and stagger[7]
  and shall be as though they had not been.

The passage expresses the principle of correspondence of sin and punishment in 15b and then illustrates it in verse 16. The talion formula appears almost exactly as it does in Lev 24:19. The correspondence of sin and punishment is then spelled out in verse 16 by repetition of the verb *šātāh*, "to drink." The shift of persons in verses 15 and 16 is confusing but not impossible to understand. Edom has been addressed in the second person singular in verses 9ff. The second person singular in 15b probably has Edom in mind and refers back to that because the nations are not addressed directly in these verses and they are spoken of in the third person plural where they are referred to. The second person plural, then, in verse 16 by context and process of elimination must refer to Judah. And the reference to drinking must surely have in mind the cup of wrath which Judah has drunk on Zion (cf. Jer 25:15ff.; Hab 2:15ff.). The conjunction *ka^{a}šer* with the perfect *š^{e}tîtem* indicating past action (v 16) is equivalent in function to the *ka'^{a}šer ʿāśîta* of v 15. It describes what the nations and Edom have done to Judah. The second colon of 16 describes in a future tense the judgment that will come upon the nations. As they made Judah drink, so they will drink. The drinking imagery as a metaphor of judgment is then elaborated in the remainder of v 16.

The talion formula and the explication of it in verse 16 make clear that the passage has as its primary intention to express the correlation of sin and

[7] The verb *lāʿû* is a *hapax legomenon*. It may mean to swallow, or it may be a textual corruption of *bāl^{e}ʿû* or *nāʿû*. Any choice is a guess. The context and parallels favor *nāʿû*.

punishment. The sentence, "Your deeds shall return on your head," in that context is somewhat ambiguous in meaning. Initially it appears to express straightforwardly the deed-result connection. But that may not necessarily be the case. The sentence is parallel to the talion statement and probably should be interpreted as indicating the same thing in another way. The fact that the next verse goes on to explicate the talion formula with a metaphor of correspondence—and one that is familiar from other passages—would tend to confirm the analysis of 15b as meaning not: "Your sins will find you out," but "You will experience the same sort of thing you dealt out to others." (Verses 10–14 would indicate more explicitly what that comparable fate will be because they catalog the sins of Edom against Judah).

Such an interpretation of *šûb* (or *hešîb*) + *g^emûl* is indicated by the other uses of this idiom. Lam 3:64 reads:

> *tāšîb lāhem g^emûl yhwh*
> *k^ema'^aśeh y^edêhem*
> You will return to them recompense, Yahweh,
> *according to* the work of their hands.

The parallel colon indicates again that the emphasis is on the correspondence of Yahweh's judgment and the sinful deeds of those against whom the complaint is raised. The same thing is indicated in Ps 28:4.

> *ten-lāhem k^epo'^olām*
> *ûk^erōa^c ma'allêhem*
> *k^ema'^aśeh y^edêhem tēn lāhem*
> *hāšēb g^emûlām lāhem*
> Give to them *according to their work*;
> and *according to the evil of their deeds*
> *According to the work* of their hands give to them;
> return *their deed* to them.

The first three cola are all parallel to each other, and one may assume the fourth says the same thing: Do to them as they have done. The idiom appears also in Ps 94:2, but the context does not clarify the question at hand as to whether it has to do primarily with correspondence or with consequence. The final example, however, places the expression again quite squarely in the context of correspondence of sin and judgment.

Joel 4:4–8

In this passage, discussed earlier, we encounter one of the most complete examples of correspondence between crime and punishment in the prophets. A translation of verses 6–8 will point that up once more:

> 6 The people of Judah and the people of Jerusalem
> you sold to the Greeks
> so as to remove them far from their territory.

7 Now I am going to rouse them up from the place
to which you sold them,
and I will bring your deed back upon your
own head (*wah^{a}šibotî g^{e}mulkem b^{e}rôš^{e}kem*).
8 I will sell your sons and daughters
into the hand of the people of Judah,
And they shall sell them to the Sabaeans
to a far off nation;
For Yahweh has spoken.

The correspondence is a complete reversal and the victim of the crime becomes the agent of judgment against the one committing the crime. Those who were sold to a far off nation will in turn sell to a far off nation those who sold them. Here is a clear case of talionic correspondence in an announcement of divine judgment. In the midst of it Yahweh explains what he is doing in this act of judgment: "I will return your deed on your head." While it is possible that such a theological statement has in mind the deed-result sequence and Yahweh's bringing into power the fateful effects of the sin, the context suggests much more clearly that Yahweh means that Tyre, Sidon, and Philistia will receive a judgment *the same as* their sin rather than the consequence of their sin.

II. *Judgment as the Consequence of the Fate-Effecting Deed.*

From the above discussion we can say that a number of passages in which the correspondence of sin and judgment is effected suggest in various ways that the judgment is found in the consequence that is worked out of the sinful deed. The judgment may be described explicitly as divine judgment or it may be formulated purely in intra-mundane terms. Even in cases where no divine initiative is indicated one may assume that God is seen as the one who brings about the consequence (e.g. Isa 1:31 and the use of *'ên m^{e}kabbeh*). But judgment or punishment seen this way focuses upon an inherent connection between a deed and the consequences that flow or grow out of it so that judgment is perceived as happening out of an order of things, not imposed from without or apart from some direct, one might say organic, relationship to the sinful deed. Your sins will find you out.

This perception of the "mechanism" of judgment is probably best conveyed in various images, some natural, some social. The image in Isa 1:31 is a good example where a strong man and his work are said to be tow and the spark that lights it so that they both burn. It is specifically "his work" that brings about the judgment. The imagery from nature and natural causes effectively conveys the consequence that comes from the deed. In Hos 7:11–12 an elaborated image of Israel as fowl and Yahweh as fowler suggests this notion as it indicates that the fowler will net the bird "as it goes." In the process of committing the sin of flying back and forth to Egypt and Assyria the bird is ensnared. The force of the deed-result connection is enhanced by describing the bird's actions as silly. Here, however, the text is explicit in ascribing the act of snaring the bird to Yahweh. The consequential fate is brought about by him as judgment. By appropriating the language of debts and pledges, Hab 2:6b–8a suggests that the deed described will surely lead to its consequences. Verses 15 and 16 depict the cup of wrath which one dispenses only to find that it has come round the table to the one who passed it out. The initiative and responsibility for judgment are at the same time the Lord's because the cup that comes round is now "in the right hand of the Lord."

Hosea provides several other examples, though perhaps not as many as Koch suggests. The agricultural images of seed and harvest are regularly interpreted in this fashion, but we have indicated above some problems in such an interpretation. The imagery of deeds surrounding the people (7:2) and possibly, but not necessarily, the statement that "their deeds do not permit them to return to Yahweh" convey the notion of wicked deeds bringing forth their consequences in judgment. So, too, inferentially rather than by imagery, it is possible to see in 4:1–3 a notion of the land languishing and dying because of or by means of the corruption in it (so Koch and Wolff). In this instance, however, it is not immediately transparent that the move from the sins of swearing, lying, killing, etc. to a judgment of land overwhelmed by drought and disappearance of animal life belongs to an inherent relationship between cause and effect. More nearly conveying that notion would be a passage like 10:13b–15 where the judgment of war (in this case not ascribed to the hand of Yahweh) is the consequence of trusting in chariots and warriors.

By analogy to this last instance it might be possible to interpret such passages as Isa 5:5–8; 28:14–18; 30:1–5, 15–16; and 31:1–3 in a similar fashion though the passages themselves do not explicitly press such an understanding.

One passage examined earlier demonstrates the way in which some texts hold in tension a deed-result connection and a more explicit notion of retribution: Deut 32:21ff. The correspondence in this poem is worked out in great detail in v 21. Yahweh's punishment corresponds to the sin in talionic fashion and by wordplay. The verses that follow depict Israel's defeat at the hands of enemies, but over and over the poem reiterates that they are only Yahweh's instrument and warns against the enemy's assumption that they accomplish the defeat on their own. Thus, the poem affirms that judgment is purely the Lord's, by his decision, and that the connection between sin and judgment is one of correspondence. The punishment is like the sin. But further in the poem where Yahweh speaks of his judgment upon Israel's enemies he says that his vengeance (*nāqām*) and recompense (*šillēm*) will be "at the time when their foot slips," i.e., judgment will be worked out of their actions.

Most or all of the above texts suggest an understanding of judgment as related to sin not by external decision but by an internal movement of cause and effect in which, as Isa 3:9b puts it, "They do to themselves evil/calamity." Judgment comes through the deed that works itself out under the power of Yahweh. Such a way of experiencing or perceiving judgment serves to emphasize the flow of human activity, the rootedness of consequences in the deeds themselves. The deed-consequence relationship was probably not so much a carefully worked out theological interpretation of the causal nexus in human events as it was a theological conclusion growing out of the experience of that relationship (and not just by scribes and sages) which was integrated with convictions about the divine activity and control of human events. Not only did God have to bring the result but there are times when it does not appear that there will be any results unless Yahweh moves and sets in motion consequences that will have the character of judgment.

III. *Judgment as the Retribution of God*

The final remark in the preceding section leads to the conclusion that one cannot fully express the relationship between sin and judgment as one of the fate-effecting deed under the guidance of God. While a number of passages do not clarify the issue one way or another, there are several which emphasize the idea of correspondence but not consequence and suggest that while there is always a causal effect in the relationship between someone or some people's actions and the judgment they receive, that relationship is not necessarily internal but is perceived as resting in the divine decision and not happening apart from that decision or decree.

Without rehearsing the previous discussion several conclusions may be drawn from the many examples presented here:

1. Some of those passages referred to by Koch as pointing to a *Tun-Ergehen Zusammenhang*, as we have seen, may be understood in a somewhat different fashion.
2. A sizeable number of judgment speeches do not suggest an internal relation between the deed and its consequence.
3. Many of these emphasize the *correspondence* of sin and punishment as the nature of the relationship rather than the *consequence*. While some of these may be understood as pointing to a judgment that could be seen as flowing out of the deed, others do not.
4. The reliance on wordplay creates a correlation that cannot be viewed as inherent in the deed. It is created or revealed only by the poetic style of the prophet.
5. To say that a punishment or judgment is *like* the sin does not necessarily point to cause and effect relationship. There is no inherent reason why consequences should be like the deeds that flow from them.
6. The emphasis upon correspondence appears to point to something other than the mechanism of cause and effect. It points rather to a concept of *retributive justice*.

One of the major reasons for Koch's objection to an idea of retribution is his assumption of the absence of a juridical character or context to statements and notions of judgment. The idea of Yahweh as judge is not involved.[8] There is no pre-established legal or judicial norm or equivalent punishment against which the deed is to be judged and punished (or rewarded). The sinful acts are not separable from the judgment that comes upon the doers. The judgment is not perceived as independent of the sin.

This construction, however, requires some modification at several points. To begin with, comparative data show that the idea that a crime leads to a punishment in the sense of the punishment being a result growing out of the crime itself, i.e. the deed—result connection, can be understood quite clearly within a judicial context. In the Judicial Papyrus of Turin dated to the end of the reign of Ramses III several people are brought to the Place of Examination and tried on a charge of conspiracy.[9] The action of the court is summed up (more than once) in the following language:

> They examined them. They found them guilty. They caused their sentences to overtake them. Their crimes seized them.

The last two sentences are formulations that point strongly to the notion that punishment comes to a person out of the crime(s) he or she has committed. They fit well within the notion of the fate-effecting deed. The sentence "They caused their sentences to overtake them," correlates with Koch's view of Yahweh as the one who watches over the connection of deed and fate and completes it.[10] But all of this language here has a quite specific setting in life. It is a law court with witnesses and judges trying a case. The recognition of a connecting relationship between a crime and its punishment, a result inherent in some cases within the deed is not incompatible with a judicial setting and the intention of retribution for crimes.

Modification of Koch's assumption about the non-juridical character of judgment in the Old Testament is necessary also on the basis of the Old Testament itself. Westermann's work on the judgment speech in the prophets has pointed to a juridico-legal setting for that type of speech in which an accusation or indictment for crimes is given and a verdict rendered as an announcement of future punishment.[11] The prophet renders this as the messenger of Yahweh. While the prophetic judgment speech has its setting now in the prophetic proclamation and not the law courts, the judicial coloring is still carried. That is even more clear if the prophet is conceived of as the messenger of the court of Yahweh, as it seems to me one should do. In the

[8] Even though Yahweh is spoken of that way, as Koch acknowledges.

[9] For translations and discussion of this papyrus, see J. H. Breasted, *Ancient Records of Egypt* IV (Chicago: The University of Chicago Press, 1906–07), secs 416–53 and J. A. Wilson in ANET, 214–16 and the notes and references cited there.

[10] Koch, *Um das Prinzip der Vergeltung . . .*, 140.

[11] Westermann, *Basic Forms of Prophetic Speech*, 130–36.

court of Yahweh the divine judge renders a decision or judgment which is then carried by the messenger of the court.[12] It is difficult to conceive how one can eliminate a judicial or juridical connotation altogether from the notion of Yahweh as judge, an image that seems to lie prominently behind the judgment speech of the prophets.

The juridical character of such ways of speaking is further accented when one brings into account the correspondence element and its prominence in the judgment speeches. In the previous chapter we have suggested that this dimension also reflects a legal setting. To the extent that the forms and principle of talion are reflected in the correspondence pattern, then it presents precisely that "*äquivalente Strafe*" which Koch finds missing in the Old Testament. A pre-existent norm exists in the notion of talion. Frequently the prophets are at pains to emphasize more the likeness of the punishment to the crime than the consequence of it. That appears to be in order to stress the talionic character of it or the fact that it is retribution for *that particular* crime. The indictments or announcements of punishment do not generally refer back to legal statutes of one sort or another (with some exceptions perhaps, e.g., the possible relation of Hos 4:1–3 to the Decalogue), but in the narratives that manifest the correspondence pattern there is frequently either reference to a previous command, stipulation, or obligation that has been disobeyed, or one can discern from the act the statutes or stipulations that have been broken. Examples of the former would be Josh 7:25, referring back to 6:18–19 and 7:11–12 (there is also here clearly a sense of cause and effect, the consequence working out of the deed); 1 Sam 15:23. referring back to 15:2–3; 1 Kgs 20:42, referring back to verse 39. Examples where one can recognize the legal statutes or customs behind the sin would be 2 Sam 12:7ff. (violation of laws against adultery and murder) and 1 Kgs 21:17ff. (violation of the traditional law of inheritance and laws against murder: "Have you killed and also taken possession?").

To the extent that the covenant curses may provide a source or setting for the correspondence pattern, then here also one encounters a predetermined norm of conduct as well as a prescribed equivalent or appropriate punishment.

The study of the correspondence pattern thus serves to underscore the complexity of the Israelite understanding of judgment. Along with a strong sense of the way in which a deed sets loose a stream (Koch prefers "sphere") of consequences which affect the doer for good and ill as Yahweh brings them to effect there is also a sharp sense of judgment as retribution, negatively seen as punishment by God. There is clearly a causal dimension, but the link is made by Yahweh's decision to punish because of disobedience. The dimension of correspondence serves to do two things. It sets at the center of Yahweh's judgment the affirmation of *appropriate justice*. What

[12] Cross, *Canaanite Myth and Hebrew Epic*, 189–90.

Yahweh requires in all human beings—*mišpāṭ*. The correspondence pattern also serves to sharpen or heighten the relation between sin and punishment when the *Tun-Ergehen Zusammenhang* is not clearly evident and even when it is. By various devices for demonstrating correspondence, direct and indirect, with figures of speech and what some have called "linguistic magic" the prophet focuses the attention of addressee(s) and all others who listen in on the character of the sinful deed by announcing a punishment like unto it (whether it is an inherent consequence of it, which it may be, or not).

IV. *Judgment as purifying, reclaiming, renewing.*

The sayings of the prophets, as well as other parts of the Old Testament, know also an understanding of the purpose of divine judgment that is not only to set in effect the consequences of one's deeds or bring about an appropriate justice. There is also a clear notion of divine discipline expressed especially in the verb *ysr* and the idea of chastisement (which can be expressed in the *Tun-Ergehen* connection, see Jer 2:19). That dimension of judgment has also surfaced in some of the passages under examination here. This analysis will not attempt to explore that theme in all its manifestations or implications; instead, it will only point to three images in the passages studied that are highly functional and point to the purposive character of divine judgment.

1. A refining fire or process. (Isa 1:21ff.)
   The emphasis in this sort of imagery is not on consuming fire but on the wrath of God that smelts away the impurities of his people—their sins—refining them into the pure unalloyed metal they were meant to be and had to be to accomplish Yahweh's purposes.
2. The plumb-line or measuring line. (2 Kgs 21:10ff.)
   This image is not always seen as one that points to the renewing character of judgment, but it conveys that implicitly. It is clearly an image of judgment pointing to a norm or standard by which one may be measured, but implicitly it suggests also a "constructive" (pun intended) dimension to that judgment—to bring the wall into plumb.[13]
3. The wiped dish (2 Kgs 21:10ff.)
   In this image also the element of judgment as punishment is to the fore. But like the image of the plumb line there is a functional or utilitarian dimension that points beyond the judgment and has a larger aim than simply eliminating the food in the dish. It is in order to render the dish, which has a use or purpose, usable again, to make it clean so that Yahweh may use it according to his purpose, may fill it anew. The present food in it is spoiled and rotten. Jerusalem is the dish Yahweh will clean and use again. The image fits perfectly with the historical fate of Jerusalem—wiped clean, turned on its face to be kept till Yahweh is ready to use it once more.

[13] See the discussion of 2 Kgs 21:10ff.

V. *Judgment in the Processes of History*

One of the clear conclusions of this study is that a notion of retributive justice is not incompatible with an understanding of divine judgment wrought out in the processes of history. The correlation of sin and punishment while effected by Yahweh is not manifest in a capricious and irrational way unconnected to the nexus of events, as if it were an "act of God" in the sense that insurance companies use such a term, a bolt of lightning from the sky that suddenly destroys. There is no such trivialization of the notion of judgment in the passages studied. On the contrary, they reveal a kind of synergism in which divine and human action are forged into a single whole or the divine intention of judgment is wrought out through human agency. Rarely does the punishment or judgment happen immediately when it is pronounced. The prophet declares Yahweh's will, which in and through the coming events will work itself out. Isaiah's oracles especially underscore this. When he speaks in Yahweh's name about Assyria as "the rod of my anger" he bears testimony to the fact that the context in which punishment takes place is provided by God. One may speak about Sennacherib's destruction of the cities of Judah, Nebuchadnezzar's siege of Jerusalem, or Shalmaneser's capture of Samaria, but such language does not exhaust the reality unveiled by the prophets, nor does it in any sense reveal the character of these events as the judgment of God. The prophetic announcement is that Sennacherib's encampment against Jerusalem is Yahweh's encampment. The act of war is an act of judgment. The latter does not run counter to the historical processes but happens within them. The meaning and happening, however, are not properly perceived until one recognizes that Yahweh has brought about this announced judgment.

For the individual who comes under judgment the same is true. No matter how closely the punishment is correlated with the sin or whether the deed-result connection is emphasized or not, the punishment is effected and wrought out in the course of the individual's life. Frequently the individual judgment is part of the larger national judgment, as for example in the case of the priest of Bethel, Amaziah, whose punishment is intimately tied to the office he has used to oppose the divine will. But the multi-faceted "depriesting" of Amaziah takes place in and as a part of the judgment that God brings against the nation as a whole. The adversities of David in the latter half of the Books of Samuel are only perceived as divine judgment when one hears the prior prophetic word of Nathan correlating the sin with the punishment. At times the correlation of punishment with crime only happens as a specific symbolic action is taken to turn the event of war, the death of an enemy or the like into the fulfillment of a prophetic word of judgment. A case in point is Jehu's casting of the body of Joram onto the plot of ground formerly owned by Naboth the Jezreelite.

So the prophets declared a poetic justice, not only seeing in the events of the future the enactment of Yahweh's decree of judgment, but frequently perceiving an appropriateness of the punishment to the crime. This correlation did not run counter to the course of events. It was God's retribution within that context and its appropriateness was manifest in diverse ways. There remains a mystery to this interaction of divine act and human agency behind which one cannot go, but its reality and centrality for the prophetic word are always assumed. The theological task is not to eliminate this word of judgment in history but to probe more deeply into understanding that reality past and present, for only in this way can the message of the prophets come to life and perdure.

BIBLIOGRAPHY

Albright, W. F. "Some Remarks on the Song of Moses in Deuteronomy XXXII," *VT* 9 (1959) 339–46.

Avishur, Y. "Pairs of Synonymous Words in the Construct State (and in Appositional Hendiadys) in Biblical Hebrew," *Semitics* 2 (1971–72) 17–81.

Bach, R. *Die Aufforderungen zur Flucht und zum Kampf im Alttestamentlichen Prophetenspruch*, WMANT, 9. Neukirchen-Vluyn: Neukirchener Verlag, 1962.

Bright, J. "Isaiah-I." *Peake's Commentary on the Bible*. London: Thomas Nelson and Sons, 1962.

———. *Jeremiah*. Anchor Bible. Garden City, N.J.: Doubleday and Company, 1965.

Brueggemann, W. *The Land*. Philadelphia: Fortress Press, 1977.

Cardascia, G. *Les Lois Assyriennes*, "Litteratures anciennes du Proche-Orient." Paris: Les Éditions du Cerf, 1969.

Cross, F. M. *Canaanite Myth and Hebrew Epic*. Cambridge: Harvard University Press, 1973.

Dahood, M. *Psalms III*. Anchor Bible. Garden City, N.J.: Doubleday and Company, 1970.

Donner, H. *Israel unter den Völker*. Supplements to *Vetus Testamentum*. Leiden: E. J. Brill, 1964.

Donner, H. and Röllig, W. *Kanaanäische und Aramäische Inschriften*, 3 vols. Wiesbaden: O. Harrassowitz, 1964.

Dossin, G. "Une revelation du dieu Dagan a Terqa," *Revue d'Assyriologie* 42 (1948) 128–32.

Driver, G. R. "'Another Little Drink'—Isaiah 28:1–22." *Words and Meanings*, ed. by P. R. Ackroyd and B. Lindars. Cambridge: Cambridge University Press, 1968, 47–67.

Driver, G. R. and Miles, J. *The Assyrian Laws*. Oxford: Oxford University Press, 1935.

———. *The Babylonian Laws*. 2 vols. Oxford: Oxford University Press, 1952–55.

Eichrodt, W. *Ezekiel*. The Old Testament Library. Philadelphia: The Westminster Press, 1970.

Eissfeldt, O. *Das Lied Moses Deut. 32:1–43 und das Lehrgedicht Asaphs Psalm 78 samt einer Analyse der Umgebung des Mose-Liedes.* Berichte über die Verhandlungen der Sachsischen Akademie der Wissenschaften zu Leipzig, Philologisch-historisch Klasse, Band 104, Heft 5, 1958.

Fichtner, J. "Jesaja unter den Weisen," *ThLZ* 74 (1949) 75–80.

Freedman, D. N. "Divine Names and Titles in Early Hebrew Poetry," *Magnalia Dei: The Mighty Acts of God*, ed. by F. M. Cross, W. E. Lemke, and P. D. Miller, Jr. Garden City, N.J.: Doubleday and Company, 1976.

Harper, W. R. *Amos and Isaiah.* ICC. Edinburgh: T. & T. Clark, 1905.

Hillers, D. *Treaty Curses and the Old Testament Prophets.* Biblica et Orientalia. Rome: Pontifical Biblical Institute, 1964.

Jackson, B. S. "The Problem of Exodus 21:22–25 (ius talionis)." *Essays in Jewish and Comparative Legal History.* Leiden: E. J. Brill, 1975.

Jacobsen, T. *The Treasures of Darkness.* New Haven: Yale University Press, 1975.

Janzen, W. *Mourning Cry and Woe Oracle.* BZAW 125. Berlin & New York: Walter de Gruyter, 1972.

Kaiser, O. *Isaiah 13–29.* The Old Testament Library. Philadelphia: The Westminster Press, 1974.

Koch, K. "Gibt es ein Vergeltungsdogma im Alten Testament?" *ZThK* 52 (1955) 1–42 (Reprinted in *Um das Prinzip der Vergeltung in Religion und Recht des Alten Testaments*, 130–80.)

__________. ed. *Um das Princip der Vergeltung in Religion und Recht des Alten Testaments.* Darmstadt: Wissenschaftliche Buchgesellschaft, 1972.

Lichtenstein, M. "The Poetry of Poetic Justice: A Comparative Study in Biblical Imagery," *JANES* 5 (1973) 255–65.

Lindblom, J. *Micha literarisch untersucht.* Abo: Akademi, 1929.

__________. "A Study on the Immanuel Section in Isaiah." *Scripta Minora Regiae Societatis Humaniorum Litterarum Lundensis*, 4, 1957–58.

Lohfink, N. "Zu Text und Form von Os 4, 4–6," *Biblica* 42 (1961) 303–32,

Mays, J. L. *Amos.* The Old Testament Library. Philadelphia: The Westminster Press, 1969.

__________. *Hosea.* The Old Testament Library. Philadelphia: The Westminster Press, 1969.

__________. *Micah.* The Old Testament Library. Philadelphia: The Westminster Press, 1976.

Miller, P. D. and Roberts, J. J. M. *The Hand of the Lord: A Reassessment of the "Ark Narrative" of I Samuel.* Baltimore: The Johns Hopkins University Press, 1977.

__________. "The Divine Council and the Prophetic Call to War," *VT* 18 (1968) 100–7.

Noth, M. *Das Buch Josua.* Handbuch zum Alten Testament. Tübingen: J. C. B. Mohr, 1953.

Preiser, W. "Vergeltung und Sühne im altisraelitischen Strafrecht," *Um das Prinzip der Vergeltung in Religion und Recht des Alten Testaments*. ed. by K. Koch. Darmstadt: Wissenschaftliche Buchgesellschaft, 1972, 236–77.

Pritchard, J. B. ed. *Ancient Near Eastern Texts Relating to the Old Testament*. Princeton: Princeton University Press, 1955 (2nd edition), 1968 (3rd edition).

Riemann, P. *Desert and Return to Desert in the Pre-Exilic Prophets*. Unpublished Ph.D. Dissertation, Harvard University, 1964.

Robertson, D. A. *Linguistic Evidence in the Dating of Early Hebrew Poetry*. SBL Dissertation Series. Missoula, Montana: Scholars Press, 1972.

Rudolph, W. *Hosea*. Kommentar zum Alten Testament. Gerd Mohn: Gutersloher Verlagshaus, 1966.

Scharbert, J. "SLM im Alten Testament," *Um das Prinzip der Vergeltung in Religion und Recht des Alten Testaments*, ed. by K. Koch, Darmstadt: Wissenschaftliche Buchgesellschaft, 1972, 300–24.

Tsevat, M. "Studies in the Book of Samuel," *HUCA* 32 (1961), 191–216.

Weissmann, J. "Talion und öffentliche Strafe im Mosäischen Rechte," *Um das Prinzip der Vergeltung in Religion und Recht des Alten Testaments*, ed. by K. Koch, Darmstadt: Wissenschaftliche Buchgesellschaft, 1972, 325–406.

Westermann, C. *Basic Forms of Prophetic Speech*. Philadelphia: The Westminster Press, 1967.

Wildberger, H. *Jesaja*, Biblischer Kommentar, Altes Testament. Neukirchen-Vluyn: Neukirchener Verlag, 1972–.

Wolff, H. W. "Die Begründungen der prophetischen Heils-und Unheilsprüche," *ZAW* 52 (1934), 1–22. (Reprinted in *Gesammelte Studien zum Alten Testament*. Munchen: Chr. Kaiser Verlag, 1973, 9–35.)

__________. *Hosea*. Hermeneia. Philadelphia: Fortress Press, 1974.

__________. *Joel and Amos*. Hermeneia. Philadelphia: Fortress Press, 1977.

Wright, G. E. "The Lawsuit of God: A Form-Critical Study of Deuteronomy 32," *Israel's Prophetic Heritage*, ed. by B. W. Anderson and W. Harrelson. New York: Harper & Brothers, 1962, 26–67.

Zimmerli, W. *Ezechiel 25–48*. Biblischer Kommentar, Altes Testament. Neukirchen-Vluyn: Neukirchener Verlag, 1969.

__________. "Verkündigung und Sprache der Botschaft Jesajas," *Studien zur Alttestamentlichen Theologie und Prophetie*. München: Chr. Kaiser Verlag, 1974, 73–87.